AWAKENED IMAGINATION
AND
FREEDOM FOR ALL

Neville Goddard

CLASSY
PUBLISHING

AWAKENED IMAGINATION AND FREEDOM FOR ALL
by Neville Goddard

Published by Classy Publishing, 2024

www.classypublishing.com
info@classypublishing.com

ISBN: 978-93-5522-739-3

No part of this publication may be reproduced, stored in a retrieval system, or transmitted, in any form or by any means, electronic, mechanical, photocopying, recording or otherwise, without the prior permission of the publisher.

Cover Image by Friedbert / Adobe Stock
Cover Design by Classy Publishing

CONTENTS

AWAKENED IMAGINATION

1.	Who Is Your Imagination?	5
2.	Sealed Instructions	12
3.	Highways of the Inner World	21
4.	The Pruning Shears of Revision	27
5.	The Coin of Heaven	34
6.	It Is Within	44
7.	Creation Is Finished	49
8.	The Apple of God's Eye	56

FREEDOM FOR ALL

1.	The Oneness of God	63
2.	The Name of God	68
3.	The Law of Creation	72
4.	The Secret of Feeling	75
5.	The Sabbath	82
6.	Healing	88
7.	Desire, the Word of God	92
8.	Faith	98
9.	The Annunciator	101

AWAKENED IMAGINATION

Imagination, the real and eternal world of which this Vegetable Universe is but a faint shadow. What is the life of Man but Art and Science?
—William Blake, Jerusalem

Imagination is more important than knowledge.
—Albert Einstein, On Science

CHAPTER 1

Who Is Your Imagination?

*I rest not from my great task
To open the Eternal Worlds,
to open the immortal Eyes
Of Man inwards into the Worlds of Thought:
into Eternity
Ever expanding in the Bosom of
God, the Human Imagination.*

—Blake, Jerusalem 5:18-20

Certain words in the course of long use gather so many strange connotations that they almost cease to mean anything at all. Such a word is imagination. This word is made to serve all manner of ideas, some of them directly opposed to one another. Fancy, thought, hallucination, suspicion: indeed, so wide is its use and so varied its meanings, the word imagination has no status nor fixed significance.

For example, we ask a man to "use his imagination", meaning that his present outlook is too restricted and therefore not equal to the task. In the next breath, we tell him that his ideas are "pure imagination", thereby implying that his ideas are unsound. We speak of a jealous or suspicious person as a "victim of his own imagination", meaning that his thoughts are untrue. A minute later we pay a man the highest tribute by describing him as a "man of imagination".

Thus the word imagination has no definite meaning. Even the dictionary gives us no help. It defines imagination as (1) the picturing power or act of the mind, the constructive or creative principle; (2) a phantasm; (3) an irrational notion or belief; (4) planning, plotting or scheming as involving mental construction.

I identify the central figure of the Gospels with human imagination, the power which makes the forgiveness of sins, the achievement of our goals, inevitable.

All things were made by Him; and without Him was not anything made that was made.

—John 1:3

There is only one thing in the world, Imagination, and all our deformations of it.

He is despised and rejected of men; a man of sorrows, and acquainted with grief.

—Isaiah 53:3

Imagination is the very gateway of reality.

"Man", said Blake, "is either the ark of God or a phantom of the earth and of the water". "Naturally he is only a natural organ subject to Sense". "The Eternal Body of Man is The Imagination: that is God himself, The Divine Body. [yod, shin, ayin; from right to the left]: Jesus: we are His Members".

I know of no greater and truer definition of the Imagination than that of Blake. By imagination we have the power to be anything we desire to be.

"Through imagination, we disarm and transform the violence of the world. Our most intimate as well as our most casual relationships become imaginative, as we awaken to "the mystery hid from the ages" [Colossians 1:26], that Christ in us is our imagination."

We then realize that only as we live by imagination can we truly be said to live at all.

I want this book to be the simplest, clearest, frankest work I have the power to make it, that I may encourage you to function imaginatively, that you may open your "Immortal Eyes inwards into the Worlds of Thought" [William Blake], where you behold every desire of your heart as ripe grain "white already to harvest" [John 4:35].

I am come that they might have life, and that they might have it more abundantly.
—John 10:10

The abundant life that Christ promised us is ours to experience now, but not until we have the sense of Christ as our imagination can we experience it.

"The mystery hid from the ages… Christ in you, the hope of glory" [Colossians 1:26,27] is your imagination.

This is the mystery which I am ever striving to realize more keenly myself and to urge upon others.

Imagination is our redeemer, "the Lord from Heaven" born of man but not begotten of man [The Nicene-Constantinopolitan Creed or the Symbol of Faith, 325/381 A.D.].

Every man is Mary and birth to Christ must give.

If the story of the immaculate conception and birth of Christ appears irrational to man, it is only because it is misread as biography, history, and cosmology, and the modern explorers of the imagination do not help by calling It the unconscious or subconscious mind.

Imagination's birth and growth is the gradual transition from a God of tradition to a God of experience. If the birth of Christ in man seems slow, it is only because man is unwilling to let go the comfortable but false anchorage of tradition.

When imagination is discovered as the first principle of religion, the stone of literal understanding will have felt the rod of Moses and, like the rock of Zion [Isaiah 28:16; Romans 9:33], issue forth the water of psychological meaning to quench the thirst of humanity;

and all who take the proffered cup and live a life according to this truth will transform the water of psychological meaning into the wine of forgiveness. Then, like the good Samaritan [Luke 10:33-35], they will pour it on the wounds of all.

The Son of God is not to be found in history, nor in any external form. He can only be found as the imagination of him in whom His presence becomes manifest.

"O, would thy heart but be a manger for His birth! God would once more become a child on earth. [Angelus Silesius, a 17th century poet]

Man is the garden in which this only-begotten Son of God sleeps. He awakens this Son by lifting his imagination up to heaven and clothing men in godlike stature. We must go on imagining better than the best we know.

Man in the moment of his awakening to the imaginative life must meet the test of Sonship.

Father, reveal Thy Son in me

—James Montgomery

and

It pleased God to reveal His Son in me

—Galatians 1:15,16

The supreme test of Sonship is the forgiveness of sin. The test that your imagination is Christ Jesus, the Son of God, is your ability to forgive sin. Sin means missing one's mark in life, falling short of one's ideal, failing to achieve one's aim. Forgiveness means identification of man with his ideal or aim in life. This is the work of awakened imagination, the supreme work, for it tests man's ability to enter into and partake of the nature of his opposite.

Let the weak man say, I am strong

—Joel 3:10

Reasonably, this is impossible. Only awakened imagination can enter into and partake of the nature of its opposite.

This conception of Christ Jesus as human imagination raises these fundamental questions: Is imagination a power sufficient, not merely to enable me to assume that I am strong, but is it also of itself capable of executing the idea?

Suppose that I desire to be in some other place or situation. Could I, by imagining myself into such a state and place, bring about their physical realization? Suppose I could not afford the journey and suppose my present social and financial status oppose the idea that I want to realize. Would imagination be sufficient of itself to incarnate these desires? Does imagination comprehend reason? By reason, I mean deductions from the observations of the senses.

Does it recognize the external world of facts? In the practical way of everyday life is imagination a complete guide to behaviour?

Suppose I am capable of acting with continuous imagination, that is, suppose I am capable of sustaining the feeling of my wish fulfilled, will my assumption harden into fact?

And, if it does harden into fact, shall I on reflection find that my actions through the period of incubation have been reasonable? Is my imagination a power sufficient, not merely to assume the feeling of the wish fulfilled, but is it also of itself capable of incarnating the idea?

After assuming that I am already what I want to be, must I continually guide myself by reasonable ideas and actions in order to bring about the fulfillment of my assumption?

Experience has convinced me that an assumption, though false, if persisted in, will harden into fact, that continuous imagination is sufficient for all things, and all my reasonable plans and actions will never make up for my lack of continuous imagination.

Is it not true that the teachings of the Gospels can only be received in terms of faith and that the Son of God is constantly looking for signs of faith in people – that is, faith in their own imagination?

Is not the promise "Believe that ye receive and ye shall receive", Mark 11:24, "the same as "Imagine that you are and you shall be"? Was it not an imaginary state in which Moses "Endured, as seeing Him who is invisible" [Hebrews 11:27]?

Was it not by the power of his own imagination that he endured?

Truth depends upon the intensity of the imagination, not upon external facts. Facts are the fruit bearing witness of the use or misuse of the imagination.

Man becomes what he imagines. He has a self-determined history. Imagination is the way, the truth, the life revealed.

We cannot get hold of truth with the logical mind. Where the natural man of sense sees a bud, imagination sees a rose full-blown.

Truth cannot be encompassed by facts.

As we awaken to the imaginative life, we discover that to imagine a thing is to make it so, that a true judgment need not conform to the external reality to which it relates.

The imaginative man does not deny the reality of the sensuous outer world of Becoming, but he knows that it is the inner world of continuous Imagination that is the force by which the sensuous outer world of Becoming is brought to pass. He sees the outer world and all its happenings as projections of the inner world of Imagination.

To him, everything is a manifestation of the mental activity which goes on in man's imagination, without the sensuous reasonable man being aware of it.

But he realizes that every man must become conscious of this inner activity and see the relationship between the inner causal world of imagination and the sensuous outer world of effects.

It is a marvelous thing to find that you can imagine yourself into the state of your fulfilled desire and escape from the jails which ignorance built.

The Real Man is a Magnificent Imagination. It is this self that must be awakened.

Awake thou that sleepest, and arise from the dead, and Christ shall give thee light.

—Ephesians 5:14

The moment man discovers that his imagination is Christ, he accomplishes acts which on this level can only be called miraculous. But until man has the sense of Christ as his imagination - "You did not choose me, I have chosen you" [John 15:16] - he will see everything in pure objectivity without any subjective relationship."

Not realizing that all that he encounters is part of himself, he rebels at the thought that he has chosen the conditions of his life, that they are related by affinity to his own mental activity.

Man must firmly come to believe that reality lies within him and not without.

Although others have bodies, a life of their own, their reality is rooted in you, ends in you, as yours ends in God.

CHAPTER 2

Sealed Instructions

The first power that meets us at the threshold of the soul's domain is the power of imagination.
—Dr. Franz Hartmann

I was first made conscious of the power, nature, and redemptive function of imagination through the teachings of my friend Abdullah; and through subsequent experiences, I learned that Jesus was a symbol of the coming of imagination to man, that the test of His birth in man was the individual's ability to forgive sin; that is, his ability to identify himself or another with his aim in life.

Without the identification of man with his aim, the forgiveness of sin is an impossibility, and only the Son of God can forgive sin.

Therefore, man's ability to identify himself with his aim, though reason and his senses deny it, is proof of the birth of Christ in him.

To passively surrender to appearances and bow before the evidence of facts is to confess that Christ is not yet born in you.

Although this teaching shocked and repelled me at first – for I was a convinced and earnest Christian, and did not then know that Christianity could not be inherited by the mere accident of birth but must be consciously adopted as a way of life – it stole later on, through visions, mystical revelations, and practical experiences, into my understanding and found its interpretation in a deeper mood. But I must confess that it is a trying time when those things are shaken which one has always taken for granted.

> *Seest thou these great buildings? There shall not be left one stone upon another that shall not be thrown down.*
> —Mark 13:2

Not one stone of literal understanding will be left after one drinks the water of psychological meaning.

All that has been built up by natural religion is cast into the flames of mental fire. Yet, what better way is there to understand Christ Jesus than to identify the central character of the Gospels with human imagination – knowing that, every time you exercise your imagination lovingly on behalf of another, you are literally mediating God to man and thereby feeding and clothing Christ Jesus and that, whenever you imagine evil against another, you are literally beating and crucifying Christ Jesus?

Every imagination of man is either the cup of cold water or the sponge of vinegar to the parched lips of Christ.

"Let none of you imagine evil in your hearts against his neighbor", warned the prophet Zechariah [8:17].

When man heeds this advice, he will awake from the imposed sleep of Adam into the full consciousness of the Son of God. He is in the world, and the world is made by Him, and the world knows Him not [Approx., John 1:10]: Human Imagination.

I asked myself many times, "If my imagination is Christ Jesus and all things are possible to Christ Jesus, are all things possible to me?"

Through experience, I have come to know that, when I identify myself with my aim in life, then Christ is awake in me.

"Christ is sufficient for all things. ["For in Him dwelleth all the fullness of the Godhead bodily, And ye are complete in Him, which is the head of all principality and power", Colossians 2:9,10; "My grace is sufficient for thee", 2 Corinthians 12:9]

I lay down My life that I might take it again. No man taketh it from Me, but I lay it down of Myself.
—John 10:17,18

What a comfort it is to know that all that I experience is the result of my own standard of beliefs; that I am the center of my own web of circumstances and that as I change, so must my outer world!

The world presents different appearances according as our states of consciousness differ.

What we see when we are identified with a state cannot be seen when we are no longer fused with it.

By state is meant all that man believes and consents to as true.

No idea presented to the mind can realize itself unless the mind accepts it.

It depends on the acceptance, the state with which we are identified, how things present themselves. In the fusion of imagination and states is to be found the shaping of the world as it seems. The world is a revelation of the states with which imagination is fused. It is the state from which we think that determines the objective world in which we live. The rich man, the poor man, the good man, the thief are what they are by virtue of the states from which they view the world. On the distinction between these states depends the distinction between the worlds of these men. Individually so different is this same world. It is not the actions and behaviour of the good man that should be matched but his point of view.

Outer reforms are useless if the inner state is not changed.

Success is gained not by imitating the outer actions of the successful but by right inner actions and inner talking.

If we detach ourselves from a state, and we may at any moment, the conditions and circumstances to which that union gave being vanish.

It was in the fall of 1933 in New York City that I approached Abdullah with a problem. He asked me one simple question, "What do you want?"

I told him that I would like to spend the winter in Barbados, but that I was broke. I literally did not have a nickel.

"If you will imagine yourself to be in Barbados", said he, "thinking and viewing the world from that state of consciousness instead of thinking of Barbados, you will spend the winter there.

You must not concern yourself with the ways and means of getting there, for the state of consciousness of already being in Barbados, if occupied by your imagination, will devise the means best suited to realize itself."

Man lives by committing himself to invisible states, by fusing his imagination with what he knows to be other than himself, and in this union he experiences the results of that fusion. No one can lose what he has, save by detachment from the state where the things experienced have their natural life.

"You must imagine yourself right into the state of your fulfilled desire", Abdullah told me, "and fall asleep viewing the world from Barbados."

The world which we describe from observation must be as we describe it relative to ourselves.

Our imagination connects us with the state desired.

But we must use imagination masterfully, not as an onlooker thinking of the end, but as a partaker thinking from the end.

We must actually be there in imagination.

If we do this, our subjective experience will be realized objectively.

"This is not mere fancy", said he, "but a truth you can prove by experience."

His appeal to enter into the wish fulfilled was the secret of thinking from the end. Every state is already there as "mere possibility" as long as you think of it, but is overpoweringly real when you think from it. Thinking from the end is the way of Christ.

I began right there and then, fixing my thoughts beyond the limits of sense, beyond that aspect to which my present state gave being, towards the feeling of already being in Barbados and viewing the world from that standpoint.

He emphasized the importance of the state from which man views the world as he falls asleep. All prophets claim that the voice of God is chiefly heard by man in dreams.

> *In a dream, in a vision of the night, when deep sleep falleth upon men, in slumbering upon the bed; then he openeth the ears of men, and sealeth their instruction.*
> —Job 33:15,16

That night and for several nights thereafter, I fell asleep in the assumption that I was in my father's house in Barbados. Within a month, I received a letter from my brother, saying that he had a strong desire to have the family together at Christmas and asking me to use the enclosed steamship ticket for Barbados. I sailed two days after I received my brother's letter and spent a wonderful winter in Barbados.

This experience has convinced me that man can be anything he pleases if he will make the conception habitual and think from the end.

It has also shown me that I can no longer excuse myself by placing the blame on the world of external things – that my good and my evil have no dependency except from myself – that it depends on the state from which I view the world how things present themselves.

Man, who is free in his choice, acts from conceptions which he freely, though not always wisely, chooses. All conceivable states are awaiting our choice and occupancy, but no amount of rationalizing will of itself yield us the state of consciousness which is the only thing worth having.

The imaginative image is the only thing to seek.

The ultimate purpose of imagination is to create in us "the spirit of Jesus", which is continual forgiveness of sin, continual identification of man with his ideal.

Only by identifying ourselves with our aim can we forgive ourselves for having missed it. All else is labor in vain. On this path, to whatever place or state we convey our imagination, to that place or state we will gravitate physically also."

In My Father's house are many mansions; if it were not so, I would have told you. I go to prepare a place for you. And if I go and prepare a place for you, I will come again, and receive you unto Myself; that where I am, there ye may be also.
—John 14:2,3

By sleeping in my father's house in my imagination as though I slept there in the flesh, I fused my imagination with that state and was compelled to experience that state in the flesh also.

So vivid was this state to me, I could have been seen in my father's house had any sensitive entered the room where in imagination I was sleeping. A man can be seen where in imagination he is, for a man must be where his imagination is, for his imagination is himself. This I know from experience, for I have been seen by a few to whom I desired to be seen, when physically I was hundreds of miles away.

I, by the intensity of my imagination and feeling, imagining and feeling myself to be in Barbados instead of merely thinking of Barbados, had spanned the vast Atlantic to influence my brother into desiring my presence to complete the family circle at Christmas.

Thinking from the end, from the feeling of my wish fulfilled, was the source of everything that happened as outer cause, such as my brother's impulse to send me a steamship ticket; and it was also the cause of everything that appeared as results.

In Ideas of Good and Evil, W. B. Yeats, having described a few experiences similar to this experience of mine, writes:

"If all who have described events like this have not dreamed, we should rewrite our histories, for all men, certainly all imaginative men, must be forever casting forth enchantments, glamour, illusions; and all men, especially tranquil men who have no powerful egotistic life, must be continually passing under their power."

Determined imagination, thinking from the end, is the beginning of all miracles.

I would like to give you an immense belief in miracles, but a miracle is only the name given by those who have no knowledge of the power and function of imagination to the works of imagination.

Imagining oneself into the feeling of the wish fulfilled is the means by which a new state is entered. This gives the state the quality of is-ness.

Hermes tells us:

That which is, is manifested; that which has been or shall be, is unmanifested, but not dead; for Soul, the eternal activity of God, animates all things.

The future must become the present in the imagination of the one who would wisely and consciously create circumstances.

We must translate vision into Being, thinking of into thinking from. Imagination must center itself in some state and view the world from that state. Thinking from the end is an intense perception of the world of fulfilled desire.

Thinking from the state desired is creative living. Ignorance of this ability to think from the end is bondage.

It is the root of all bondage with which man is bound. To passively surrender to the evidence of the senses underestimates the capacities of the Inner Self.

Once man accepts thinking from the end as a creative principle in which he can cooperate, then he is redeemed from the absurdity of ever attempting to achieve his objective by merely thinking of it.

Construct all ends according to the pattern of fulfilled desire.

The whole of life is just the appeasement of hunger, and the infinite states of consciousness from which a man can view the world are purely a means of satisfying that hunger.

The principle upon which each state is organized is some form of hunger to lift the passion for self-gratification to ever higher and higher levels of experience.

Desire is the mainspring of the mental machinery. It is a blessed thing. It is a right and natural craving which has a state of consciousness as its right and natural satisfaction.

> *But one thing I do, forgetting the things which are behind, and stretching forward to the things which are before, I press on toward the goal.*
>
> —Philippians 3:13,14

It is necessary to have an aim in life. Without an aim, we drift. "What wantest thou of Me?" [What wilt thou that I shall do unto thee? Luke 18:41] is the implied question asked most often by the central figure of the Gospels. In defining your aim, you must want it.

> *As the hart panteth after the water brooks, so panteth my soul after Thee, O, God.*
>
> —Psalms 42:1

It is lack of this passionate direction to life that makes man fail of accomplishment.

The spanning of the bridge between desire – thinking of – and satisfaction – thinking from – is all-important.

We must move mentally from thinking of the end to thinking from the end.

This, reason could never do. By its nature, it is restricted to the evidence of the senses; but imagination, having no such limitation, can.

Desire exists to be gratified in the activity of imagination.

Through imagination, man escapes from the limitation of the senses and the bondage of reason.

There is no stopping the man who can think from the end. Nothing can stop him. He creates the means and grows his way out of limitation into ever greater and greater mansions of the Lord.

It does not matter what he has been or what he is. All that matters is "what does he want?"

He knows that the world is a manifestation of the mental activity which goes on within himself, so he strives to determine and control the ends from which he thinks.

In his imagination he dwells in the end, confident that he shall dwell there in the flesh also.

He puts his whole trust in the feeling of the wish fulfilled and lives by committing himself to that state, for the art of fortune is to tempt him so to do.

Like the man at the pool of Bethesda, he is ready for the moving of the waters of imagination.

Knowing that every desire is ripe grain to him who knows how to think from the end, he is indifferent to mere reasonable probability and confident that through continuous imagination his assumptions will harden into fact.

But how to persuade men everywhere that thinking from the end is the only living, how to foster it in every activity of man, how to reveal it as the plenitude of life and not the compensation of the disappointed: that is the problem.

Life is a controllable thing.

You can experience what you please once you realize that you are His Son, and that you are what you are by virtue of the state of consciousness from which you think and view the world,

Son, Thou art ever with Me, and all that I have is Thine.
—Luke 15:31

CHAPTER 3

Highways of the Inner World

And the children struggled within her... and the Lord said unto her, two nations are in thy womb, and two manner of people shall be separated from thy bowels; and the one people shall be stronger than the other people; and the elder shall serve the younger.

—Genesis 25:22,23

Duality is an inherent condition of life. Everything that exists is double. Man is a dual creature with contrary principles embedded in his nature. They war within him and present attitudes to life which are antagonistic. This conflict is the eternal enterprise, the war in heaven, the never-ending struggle of the younger or inner man of imagination to assert His supremacy over the elder or outer man of sense.

The first shall be last and the last shall be first.

—Matthew 19:30

He it is, Who coming after me is preferred before me.

—John 1:27

The second Man is the Lord from heaven.

—1 Corinthians 15:47

Man begins to awake to the imaginative life the moment he feels the presence of another being in himself.

In your limbs lie nations twain, rival races from their birth; one the mastery shall gain, the younger o'er the elder reign.

There are two distinct centers of thought or outlooks on the world possessed by every man.

The Bible speaks of these two outlooks as natural and spiritual.

> *The natural man receiveth not the things of the Spirit of God: for they are foolishness unto him: neither can he know them, because they are spiritually discerned.*
> —1 Corinthians 2:14

Man's inner body is as real in the world of subjective experience as his outer physical body is real in the world of external realities, but the inner body expresses a more fundamental part of reality.

This existing inner body of man must be consciously exercised and directed.

The inner world of thought and feeling to which the inner body is attuned has its real structure and exists in its own higher space.

There are two kinds of movement, one that is according to the inner body and another that is according to the outer body. The movement which is according to the inner body is causal, but the outer movement is under compulsion. The inner movement determines the outer which is joined to it, bringing into the outer a movement that is similar to the actions of the inner body. Inner movement is the force by which all events are brought to pass. Outer movement is subject to the compulsion applied to it by the movement of the inner body.

Whenever the actions of the inner body match the actions which the outer must take to appease desire, that desire will be realized.

Construct mentally a drama which implies that your desire is realized and make it one which involves movement of self. Immobilize your outer physical self. Act precisely as though you were going to take a nap, and start the predetermined action in imagination.

A vivid representation of the action is the beginning of that action. Then, as you are falling asleep, consciously imagine yourself into the scene. The length of the sleep is not important, a short nap is sufficient, but carrying the action into sleep thickens fancy into fact.

At first your thoughts may be like rambling sheep that have no shepherd. Don't despair. Should your attention stray seventy times seven, bring it back seventy times seven to its predetermined course until from sheer exhaustion it follows the appointed path. The inner journey must never be without direction. When you take to the inner road, it is to do what you did mentally before you started. You go for the prize you have already seen and accepted.

In The Road to Xanadu, Professor John Livingston Lowes says:

"But I have long had the feeling, which this study had matured to a conviction, that Fancy and Imagination are not two powers at all, but one. The valid distinction which exists between them lies, not in the materials with which they operate, but in the degree of intensity of the operant power itself. Working at high tension, the imaginative energy assimilates and transmutes; keyed low, the same energy aggregates and yokes together those images which at its highest pitch, it merges indissolubly into one."

Fancy assembles, imagination fuses.

Here is a practical application of this theory. A year ago, a blind girl living in the city of San Francisco found herself confronted with a transportation problem. A rerouting of buses forced her to make three transfers between her home and her office. This lengthened her trip from fifteen minutes to two hours and fifteen minutes. She thought seriously about this problem and came to the decision that a car was the solution. She knew that she could not drive a car but felt that she could be driven in one. Putting this theory to the test that "whenever the actions of the inner self correspond to the actions which the outer, physical self must take to appease desire, that desire will be realized", she said to herself, "I will sit here and imagine that I am being driven to my office."

Sitting in her living room, she began to imagine herself seated in a car. She felt the rhythm of the motor. She imagined that she smelled the odor of gasoline, felt the motion of the car, touched the sleeve of the driver and felt that the driver was a man. She felt the car stop, and turning to her companion, said, "Thank you very much, sir."

To which he replied, "The pleasure is all mine."

Then she stepped from the car and heard the door snap shut as she closed it.

She told me that she centered her imagination on being in a car and, although blind, viewed the city from her imaginary ride. She did not think of the ride. She thought from the ride and all that it implied. This controlled and subjectively directed purposive ride raised her imagination to its full potency. She kept her purpose ever before her, knowing there was cohesion in purposive inner movement. In these mental journeys an emotional continuity must be sustained – the emotion of fulfilled desire. Expectancy and desire were so intensely joined that they passed at once from a mental state into a physical act.

The inner self moves along the predetermined course best when the emotions collaborate. The inner self must be fired, and it is best fired by the thought of great deeds and personal gain. We must take pleasure in our actions.

On two successive days, the blind girl took her imaginary ride, giving it all the joy and sensory vividness of reality. A few hours after her second imaginary ride, a friend told her of a story in the evening paper. It was a story of a man who was interested in the blind. The blind girl phoned him and stated her problem. The very next day, on his way home, he stopped in at a bar and while there had the urge to tell the story of the blind girl to his friend the proprietor. A total stranger, on hearing the story, volunteered to drive the blind girl home every day. The man who told the story then said, "If you will take her home, I will take her to work."

This was over a year ago, and since that day, this blind girl has been driven to and from her office by these two gentlemen. Now, instead of spending two hours and fifteen minutes on three buses, she is at her office in less than fifteen minutes. And on that first ride to her office, she turned to her good Samaritan and said, "Thank you very much, sir"; and he replied, "The pleasure is all mine."

Thus, the objects of her imagination were to her the realities of which the physical manifestation was only the witness.

The determinative animating principle was the imaginative ride. Her triumph could be a surprise only to those who did not know of her inner ride. She mentally viewed the world from this imaginative ride with such a clearness of vision that every aspect of the city attained identity."

These inner movements not only produce corresponding outer movements: this is the law which operates beneath all physical appearances.

He who practices these exercises of bilocation will develop unusual powers of concentration and quiescence and will inevitably achieve waking consciousness on the inner and dimensionally larger world.

Actualizing strongly, she fulfilled her desire, for, viewing the city from the feeling of her wish fulfilled, she matched the state desired and granted that to herself which sleeping men ask of God.

To realize your desire, an action must start in your imagination, apart from the evidence of the senses, involving "movement of self and implying fulfillment of your desire. Whenever it is the action which the outer self takes to appease desire, that desire will be realized.

The movement of every visible object is caused not by things outside the body, but by things within it, which operate from within outward.

The journey is in yourself. You travel along the highways of the inner world. Without inner movement, it is impossible to bring forth anything. Inner action is introverted sensation. If you will construct mentally a drama which implies that you have realized your objective, then close your eyes and drop your thoughts inward, centering your imagination all the while in the predetermined action and partake in that action, you will become a self- determined being.

Inner action orders all things according to the nature of itself.

Try it and see whether a desirable ideal once formulated is possible, for only by this process of experiment can you realize your potentialities.

It is thus that this creative principle is being realized. So the clue to purposive living is to center your imagination in the action and feeling of fulfilled desire with such awareness, such sensitiveness, that you initiate and experience movement upon the inner world.

Ideas only act if they are felt, if they awaken inner movement. Inner movement is conditioned by self-motivation, outer movement by compulsion.

> *Wherever the sole of your foot shall tread, the same give I unto*
>
> —Joshua 1:3

and remember,

> *The Lord thy God in the midst of thee is mighty.*
>
> —Zephaniah 3:17

CHAPTER 4

The Pruning Shears of Revision

The second Man is the Lord from se Heaven.
—1 Corinthians 15:47

Never will he say caterpillars.
He'll say, "There's a lot of butterflies-as-is-to-be
on our cabbages, Pure."

He won't say, "It's winter."
He'll say, "Summer's sleeping."

And there's no bud little enough nor sad-coloured enough for
Kester not to callen it the beginnings of the blow.
—Mary Webb, Precious Bane

The very first act of correction or cure is always "revise". One must start with oneself. It is one's attitude that must be changed.

What we are, that only can we see.
—Emerson

It is a most healthy and productive exercise to daily relive the day as you wish you had lived it, revising the scenes to make them conform to your ideals.

For instance, suppose today's mail brought disappointing news. Revise the letter. Mentally rewrite it and make it conform to the news you wish you had received. Then, in imagination, read the revised letter over and over again. This is the essence of revision, and revision results in repeal.

The one requisite is to arouse your attention in a way and to such intensity that you become wholly absorbed in the revised action. You will experience an expansion and refinement of the senses by this imaginative exercise and eventually achieve vision.

But always remember that the ultimate purpose of this exercise is to create in you "the Spirit of Jesus", which is continual forgiveness of sin.

Revision is of greatest importance when the motive is to change oneself, when there is a sincere desire to be something different, when the longing is to awaken the ideal active spirit of forgiveness.

Without imagination, man remains a being of sin.

Man either goes forward to imagination or remains imprisoned in his senses. To go forward to imagination is to forgive. Forgiveness is the life of the imagination. The art of living is the art of forgiving.

Forgiveness is, in fact, experiencing in imagination the revised version of the day, experiencing in imagination what you wish you had experienced in the flesh.

Every time one really forgives – that is, every time one relives the event as it should have been lived – one is born again.

"Father, forgive them" is not the plea that comes once a year but the opportunity that comes every day. The idea of forgiving is a daily possibility, and, if it is sincerely done, it will lift man to higher and higher levels of being. He will experience a daily Easter, and Easter is the idea of rising transformed.

And that should be almost a continuous process.

Freedom and forgiveness are indissolubly linked.

Not to forgive is to be at war with ourselves, for we are freed according to our capacity to forgive.

> *Forgive, and you shall be forgiven.*
> —Luke 6:37

Forgive, not merely from a sense of duty or service; forgive because you want to.

> *Thy ways are ways of pleasantness and all thy paths are peace.*
> —Proverbs 3:17

You must take pleasure in revision. You can forgive others effectively only when you have a sincere desire to identify them with their ideal. Duty has no momentum.

Forgiveness is a matter of deliberately withdrawing attention from the unrevised day and giving it full strength, and joyously, to the revised day. If a man begins to revise even a little of the vexations and troubles of the day, then he begins to work practically on himself. Every revision is a victory over himself and therefore a victory over his enemy.

"A man's foes are those of his own household", Matthew 10:36, and his household is his state of mind. He changes his future as he revises his day.

When a man practices the art of forgiveness, of revision, however factual the scene on which sight then rests, he revises it with his imagination and gazes on one never before witnessed. The magnitude of the change which any act of revision involves makes such change appear wholly improbable to the realist – the unimaginative man; but the radical changes in the fortunes of the Prodigal [Luke 15:11-32] were all produced by a "change of heart".

The battle man fights is fought out in his own imagination. The man who does not revise the day has lost the vision of that life, into the likeness of which it is the true labour of the "Spirit of Jesus" to transform this life.

> *All things whatsoever ye would that men should do to you, even so do ye to them: for this is the law.*
> —Matthew 7:12

Here is the way an artist friend forgave herself and was set free from pain, annoyance and unfriendliness. Knowing that nothing but forgetfulness and forgiveness will bring us to new values, she cast herself upon her imagination and escaped from the prison of her senses. She writes:

"Thursday, I taught all day in the art school. Only one small thing marred the day. Coming into my afternoon classroom, I discovered the janitor had left all the chairs on top of the desks after cleaning the floor. As I lifted a chair down, it slipped from my grasp and struck me a sharp blow on the instep of my right foot. I immediately examined my thoughts and found that I had criticized the man for not doing his job properly. Since he had lost his helper, I realized he probably felt he had done more than enough and it was an unwanted gift that had bounced and hit me on the foot. Looking down at my foot, I saw both my skin and nylons were intact, so forgot the whole thing.

That night, after I had been working intensely for about three hours on a drawing, I decided to make myself a cup of coffee. To my utter amazement, I couldn't manage my right foot at all and it was giving out great bumps of pain. I hopped over to a chair and took off my slipper to look at it. The entire foot was a strange purplish pink, swollen out of shape and red hot. I tried walking on it and found that it just flapped. I had no control over it whatsoever. It looked like one of two things: either I had cracked a bone when I dropped the chair on it or something could be dislocated.

'No use speculating what it is. Better get rid of it right away.'

So I became quiet, all ready to melt myself into light. To my complete bewilderment, my imagination refused to cooperate. It just said 'No.'

This sort of thing often happens when I am painting. I just started to argue 'Why not?' It just kept saying 'No.'

Finally, I gave up and said, 'You know I am in pain. I am trying hard not to be frightened, but you are the boss. What do you want to do?"

"The answer: 'Go to bed and review the day's events.'

So I said 'All right. But let me tell you if my foot isn't perfect by tomorrow morning, you have only yourself to blame.'

After arranging the bed clothes so they didn't touch my foot, I started to review the day. It was slow going as I had difficulty keeping my attention away from my foot. I went through the whole day, saw nothing to add to the chair incident. But when I reached the early evening, I found myself coming face to face with a man who for the past year has made a point of not speaking. The first time this happened, I thought he had grown deaf. I had known him since school days, but we had never done more than say 'hello' and comment on the weather. Mutual friends assured me

I had done nothing, that he had said he never liked me and finally decided it was not worthwhile speaking. I had said 'Hi!'

He hadn't answered. I found that I thought 'Poor guy – what a horrid state to be in. I shall do something about this ridiculous state of affairs.'

So, in my imagination, I stopped right there and re-did the scene. I said 'Hi!' He answered 'Hi!' and smiled. I now thought 'Good old Ed.'

I ran the scene over a couple of times and went on to the next incident and finished up the day.

'Now what – do we do my foot or the concert?'

I had been melting and wrapping up a wonderful present of courage and success for a friend who was to make her debut the following day and I had been looking forward to giving it to her tonight. My imagination sounded a little bit solemn as it said 'Let us do the concert. It will be more fun.'

'But first couldn't we just take my perfectly good imagination foot out of this physical one before we start?' I pleaded. 'By all means.'

That done, I had a lovely time at the concert and my friend got a tremendous ovation.

By now I was very, very sleepy and fell asleep doing my project. The next morning, as I was putting on my slipper, I suddenly had a quick memory picture of withdrawing a discolored and swollen foot from the same slipper. I took my foot out and looked at it. It was perfectly normal in every respect. There was a tiny pink spot on the instep where I remembered I had hit it with the chair.

'What a vivid dream that was!' I thought and dressed. While waiting for my coffee, I wandered over to my drafting table and saw that all my brushes were lying helter-skelter and unwashed. 'Whatever possessed you to leave your brushes like that?'

'Don't you remember? It was because of your foot.'

So it hadn't been a dream after all, but a beautiful healing."

She had won by the art of revision what she would never have won by force.

In Heaven, the only Art of Living Is Forgetting & Forgiving. Especially to the Female.

—Blake

We should take our life, not as it appears to be, but from the vision of this artist, from the vision of the world made perfect that is buried under all minds – buried and waiting for us to revise the day.

We are led to believe a lie when we see with, not through the eye.

—Blake

A revision of the day, and what she held to be so stubbornly real was no longer so to her and, like a dream, had quietly faded away.

You can revise the day to please yourself and by experiencing in imagination the revised speech and actions not only modify the trend of your life story but turn all its discords into harmonies.

The one who discovers the secret of revision cannot do otherwise than let himself be guided by love.

Your effectiveness will increase with practice. Revision is the way by which right can find its appropriate might.

"Resist not evil" [Matthew 5:39], for all passionate conflicts result in an interchange of characteristics.

To him that knoweth to do good, and doeth it not, to him it is sin.

—James 4:17

To know the truth, you must live the truth, and to live the truth, your inner actions must match the actions of your fulfilled desire.

Expectancy and desire must become one.

Your outer world is only actualized inner movement.

Through ignorance of the law of revision, those who take to warfare are perpetually defeated.

Only concepts that idealize depict the truth.

Your ideal of man is his truest self. It is because I firmly believe that whatever is most profoundly imaginative is, in reality, most directly practical that I ask you to live imaginatively and to think into, and to personally appropriate the transcendent saying:

Christ in you, the hope of glory.

—Colossians 1:27

Don't blame; only resolve.

It is not man and the earth at their loveliest, but you practicing the art of revision make paradise.

The evidence of this truth can lie only in your own experience of it.

Try revising the day. It is to the pruning shears of revision that we owe our prime fruit.

CHAPTER 5

The Coin of Heaven

'Does a firm persuasion that a thing is so, make it so?'

And the prophet replied, 'All poets believe that it does. And in ages of imagination, this firm persuasion removed mountains: but many are not capable of a firm persuasion of anything.'
—Blake, *Marriage of Heaven and Hell*

Let every man be fully persuaded in his own mind.
—Romans 14:5

Persuasion is an inner effort of intense attention.

To listen attentively as though you heard is to evoke, to activate.

By listening, you can hear what you want to hear and persuade those beyond the range of the outer ear. Speak it inwardly in your imagination only.

Make your inner conversation match your fulfilled desire. What you desire to hear without, you must hear within.

Embrace the without within and become one who hears only that which implies the fulfillment of his desire, and all the external happenings in the world will become a bridge leading to the objective realization of your desire.

Your inner speech is perpetually written all around you in happenings.

Learn to relate these happenings to your inner speech and you will become self- taught.

By inner speech is meant those mental conversations which you carry on with yourself.

They may be inaudible when you are awake because of the noise and distractions of the outer world of becoming, but they are quite audible in deep meditation and dream.

But whether they be audible or inaudible, you are their author and fashion your world in their likeness.

> *There is a God in heaven [and heaven is within you] that revealeth secrets, and maketh known to the king Nebuchadnezzar what shall be in the latter days. Thy dream, and the visions of thy head upon thy bed, are these.*
> —Daniel 2:28

Inner speech from premises of fulfilled desire is the way to create an intelligible world for yourself.

Observe your inner speech for it is the cause of future action. Inner speech reveals the state of consciousness from which you view the world.

Make your inner speech match your fulfilled desire, for your inner speech is manifested all around you in happenings.

> *If any man offend not in word, the same is a perfect man and able also to bridle the whole body. Behold, we put bits in the horses' mouths, that they may obey us; and we turn about their whole body. Behold also the ships, which though they be so great, and are driven by fierce winds, yet are they turned about with a very small helm, whithersoever the governor listeth. Even so the tongue is a little member, and boasteth great things. Behold, how great a matter a little fire kindleth!*
> —James 3:2-5

The whole manifested world goes to show us what use we have made of the Word – Inner Speech.

An uncritical observation of our inner talking will reveal to us the ideas from which we view the world.

Inner talking mirrors our imagination, and our imagination mirrors the state with which it is fused. If the state with which we are fused is the cause of the phenomenon of our life, then we are relieved of the burden of wondering what to do, for we have no alternative but to identify ourselves with our aim, and inasmuch as the state with which we are identified mirrors itself in our inner speech, then to change the state with which we are fused, we must first change our inner talking.

It is our inner conversations which make tomorrow's facts.

Put off the former conversation, the old man, which is corrupt... and be renewed in the spirit of your mind... put on the new man, which is created in righteousness.
—Ephesians 4:22-24

Our minds, like our stomachs, are whetted by change of food.
—Quintillian

Stop all of the old mechanical negative inner talking and start a new positive and constructive inner speech from premises of fulfilled desire. Inner talking is the beginning, the sowing of the seeds of future action. To determine the action, you must consciously initiate and control your inner talking.

Construct a sentence which implies the fulfillment of your aim, such as "I have a large, steady, dependable income, consistent with integrity and mutual benefit", or "I am happily married", "I am wanted", "I am contributing to the good of the world", and repeat such a sentence over and over until you are inwardly affected by it. Our inner speech represents in various ways the world we live in.

In the beginning was the Word.

—John 1:1

That which ye sow ye reap. See yonder fields! The sesamum was sesamum, the corn was corn. The Silence and the Darkness knew! So is a man's fate born.

—Edwin Arnold, The Light of Asia

Ends run true to origins.

Those that go searching for love only make manifest their own lovelessness. And the loveless never find love, only the loving find love, and they never have to seek for it.

—D. H. Lawrence

Man attracts what he is. The art of life is to sustain the feeling of the wish fulfilled and let things come to you, not to go after them or think they flee away.

Observe your inner talking and remember your aim. Do they match?

Does your inner talking match what you would say audibly had you achieved your goal?

The individual's inner speech and actions attract the conditions of his life.

Through uncritical self-observation of your inner talking you find where you are in the inner world, and where you are in the inner world is what you are in the outer world.

You put on the new man whenever ideals and inner speech match. In this way alone can the new man be born.

Inner talking matures in the dark.

From the dark it issues into the light. The right inner speech is the speech that would be yours were you to realize your ideal. In other words, it is the speech of fulfilled desire.

I am that.
—Exodus 3:14

> *There are two gifts which God has bestowed upon man alone, and on no other mortal creature. These two are mind and speech; and the gift of mind and speech is equivalent to that of immortality. If a man uses these two gifts rightly, he will differ in nothing from the immortals... and when he quits the body, mind and speech will be his guides, and by them he will be brought into the troop of the gods and the souls that have attained to bliss.*
> —Hermetica, Walter Scott's translation

The circumstances and conditions of life are outpictured inner talking, solidified sound. Inner speech calls events into existence. In every event is the creative sound that is its life and being.

All that a man believes and consents to as true reveals itself in his inner speech. It is his Word, his life.

Try to notice what you are saying in yourself at this moment, to what thoughts and feelings you are consenting. They will be perfectly woven into your tapestry of life. To change your life, you must change your inner talking, for "life", said Hermes, "is the union of Word and Mind".

When imagination matches your inner speech to fulfilled desire, there will then be a straight path in yourself from within out, and the without will instantly reflect the within for you, and you will know reality is only actualized inner talking.

> *Receive with meekness the inborn Word which is able to save your souls.*
> —James 1:21

Every stage of man's progress is made by the conscious exercise of his imagination matching his inner speech to his fulfilled desire.

Because man does not perfectly match them, the results are uncertain, while they might be perfectly certain. Persistent assumption of the wish fulfilled is the means of fulfilling the intention.

As we control our inner talking, matching it to our fulfilled desires, we can lay aside all other processes. Then we simply act by clear imagination and intention.

We imagine the wish fulfilled and carry on mental conversations from that premise.

Through controlled inner talking from premises of fulfilled desire, seeming miracles are performed.

The future becomes the present and reveals itself in our inner speech.

To be held by the inner speech of fulfilled desire is to be safely anchored in life.

Our lives may seem to be broken by events, but they are never broken so long as we retain the inner speech of fulfilled desire.

All happiness depends on the active voluntary use of imagination to construct and inwardly affirm that we are what we want to be. We match ourselves to our ideals by constantly remembering our aim and identifying ourselves with it. We fuse with our aims by frequently occupying the feeling of our wish fulfilled.

It is the frequency, the habitual occupancy, that is the secret of success. The oftener we do it, the more natural it is. Fancy assembles. Continuous imagination fuses.

It is possible to resolve every situation by the proper use of imagination.

Our task is to get the right sentence, the one which implies that our desire is realized, and fire the imagination with it.

All this is intimately connected with the mystery of "the still small voice".

Inner talking reveals the activities of imagination, activities which are the causes of the circumstances of life.

As a rule, man is totally unaware of his inner talking and therefore sees himself not as the cause but the victim of circumstance.

To consciously create circumstance, man must consciously direct his inner speech, matching "the still small voice" to his fulfilled desires.

He calls things not seen as though they were.
—Romans 4:17

Right inner speech is essential. It is the greatest of the arts.
It is the way out of limitation into freedom.

Ignorance of this art has made the world a battlefield and penitentiary where blood and sweat alone are expected, when it should be a place of marveling and wondering."

Right inner talking is the first step to becoming what you want to be.

Speech is an image of mind, and mind is an image of God.
—Hermetica, Scott translation

On the morning of April 12, 1953, my wife was awakened by the sound of a great voice of authority speaking within her and saying, "You must stop spending your thoughts, time, and money. Everything in life must be an investment."

To spend is to waste, to squander, to layout without return. To invest is to layout for a purpose from which a profit is expected. This revelation of my wife is about the importance of the moment. It is about the transformation of the moment. What wedesire does not lie in the future but in ourselves at this very moment.

At any moment in our lives, we are faced with an infinite choice: "what we are and what we want to be".

And what we want to be is already existent, but to realize it we must match our inner speech and actions to it.

If two of you shall agree on earth as touching anything that they shall ask, it shall be done for them of My Father which is in heaven.
—Matthew 18:19

It is only what is done now that counts.

The present moment does not recede into the past. It advances into the future to confront us, spent or invested.

Thought is the coin of heaven. Money is its earthly symbol.

Every moment must be invested, and our inner talking reveals whether we are spending or investing.

Be more interested in what you are inwardly "saying now" than what you "have said" by choosing wisely what you think and what you feel now.

Any time we feel misunderstood, misused, neglected, suspicious, afraid, we are spending our thoughts and wasting our time.

Whenever we assume the feeling of being what we want to be, we are investing.

We cannot abandon the moment to negative inner talking and expect to retain command of life.

Before us go the results of all that seemingly is behind. Not gone is the last moment – but oncoming.

> *My word shall not return unto Me void, but it shall accomplish that which I please, and it shall prosper in the thing whereto I sent it.*
> —Isaiah 55:11

The circumstances of life are the muffled utterances of the inner talking that made them – the word made visible.

"The Word", said Hermes, "is Son, and the Mind is Father of the Word. They are not separate one from the other; for life is the union of Word and Mind."

> *He willed us forth from Himself by the Word of Truth.*
> —James 1:18

Let us "be imitators of God as dear children", Ephesians 5:1, and use our inner speech wisely to mould an outer world in harmony with our ideal.

> *The Lord spake by me, and His Word was in my tongue.*
> —2 Samuel 23:2

The mouth of God is the mind of man. Feed God only the best.

> *Whatsoever things are of good report... think on these things.*
> —Philippians 4:8

The present moment is always precisely right for an investment, to inwardly speak the right word.

> *The word is very near to you, in your mouth, and in your heart, that you may do it. See, I have set before you this day life and good, death and evil, blessings and cursings. Choose life.*
> —Deuteronomy 30:14,15,19

You choose life and good and blessings by being that which you choose. Like is known to like alone.

Make your inner speech bless and give good reports.

Man's ignorance of the future is the result of his ignorance of his inner talking. His inner talking mirrors his imagination, and his imagination is a government in which the opposition never comes into power.

If the reader ask, "What if the inner speech remains subjective and is unable to find an object for its love?", the answer is: it will not remain subjective, for the very simple reason that inner speech is always objectifying itself.

What frustrates and festers and becomes the disease that afflicts humanity is man's ignorance of the art of matching inner words to fulfilled desire.

Inner speech mirrors imagination, and imagination is Christ.

Alter your inner speech, and your perceptual world changes. Whenever inner speech and desire are in conflict, inner speech invariably wins.

Because inner speech objectifies itself, it is easy to see that if it matches desire, desire will be objectively realized. Were this not so, I would say with Blake:

Sooner murder an infant in its cradle than nurse unacted desires.

But I know from experience:

The tongue... setteth on fire the course of nature.
—James 3:6

CHAPTER 6

It Is Within

Rivers, Mountains, Cities, Villages,
All are Human, & when you enter into
their Bosoms you walk
In Heavens & Earths, as in your own Bosom
you bear your Heaven
And Earth & all you behold; tho' it appears
Without, it is Within,
In your Imagination, of which this
World of Mortality is but a Shadow.

—Blake, Jerusalem

The inner world was as real to Blake as the outer land of waking life. He looked upon his dreams and visions as the realities of the forms of nature. Blake reduced everything to the bedrock of his own consciousness.

The Kingdom of Heaven is within you.

—Luke 17:21

The Real Man, the Imaginative Man, has invested the outer world with all of its properties. The apparent reality of the outer world which is so hard to dissolve is only proof of the absolute reality of the inner world of his own imagination.

> *No man can come to me, except the Father which hath sent Me draw him... I and My Father are One.*
> —John 6:44; 10:30

The world which is described from observation is a manifestation of the mental activity of the observer.

When man discovers that his world is his own mental activity made visible, that no man can come unto him except he draws him, and that there is no one to change but himself, his own imaginative self, his first impulse is to reshape the world in the image of his ideal.

But his ideal is not so easily incarnated. In that moment when he ceases to conform to external discipline, he must impose upon himself a far more rigorous discipline, the self-discipline upon which the realization of his ideal depends.

Imagination is not entirely untrammeled and free to move at will without any rules to constrain it. In fact, the contrary is true. Imagination travels according to habit.

Imagination has choice, but it chooses according to habit. Awake or asleep, man's imagination is constrained to follow certain definite patterns. It is this benumbing influence of habit that man must change; if he does not, his dreams will fade under the paralysis of custom.

Imagination, which is Christ in man, is not subject to the necessity to produce only that which is perfect and good. It exercises its absolute freedom from necessity by endowing the outer physical self with free will to choose to follow good or evil, order or disorder.

> *Choose this day whom ye will serve.*
> —Joshua 24:15

But after the choice is made and accepted so that it forms the individual's habitual consciousness, then imagination manifests its infinite power and wisdom by moulding the outer sensuous world of becoming in the image of the habitual inner speech and actions of the individual.

To realize his ideal, man must first change the pattern which his imagination has followed.

Habitual thought is indicative of character.

The way to change the outer world is to make the inner speech and action match the outer speech and action of fulfilled desire.

Our ideals are waiting to be incarnated, but unless we ourselves match our inner speech and action to the speech and action of fulfilled desire, they are incapable of birth.

Inner speech and action are the channels of God's action. He cannot respond to our prayer unless these paths are offered.

The outer behaviour of man is mechanical. It is subject to the compulsion applied to it by the behaviour of the inner self, and old habits of the inner self hang on till replaced by new ones. It is a peculiar property of the second or inner man that he gives to the outer self something similar to his own reality of being. Any change in the behavior of the inner self will result in corresponding outer changes.

The mystic calls a change of consciousness "death". By death he means, not the destruction of imagination and the state with which it was fused, but the dissolution of their union.

Fusion is union rather than oneness. Thus the conditions to which that union gave being vanish. "I die daily", said Paul to the Corinthians [1 Corinthians 15:31]. Blake said to his friend Crabbe Robinson:

There is nothing like death. Death is the best thing that can happen in life; but most people die so late and take such an unmerciful time in dying. God knows, their neighbors never see them rise from the dead.

To the outer man of sense, who knows nothing of the inner man of Being, this is sheer nonsense. But Blake made the above quite clear when he wrote in the year before he died:

William Blake – one who is very much delighted with being in good company.

Born 28 November 1757 in London and has died several times since.

When man has the sense of Christ as his imagination, he sees why Christ must die and rise again from the dead to save man – why he must detach his imagination from his present state and match it to a higher concept of himself if he would rise above his present limitations and thereby save himself.

Here is a lovely story of a mystical death which was witnessed by a "neighbor".

"Last week", writes the one "who rose from the dead", "a friend offered me her home in the mountains for the Christmas holidays as she thought she might go east. She said that she would let me know this week. We had a very pleasant conversation and I mentioned you and your teaching in connection with a discussion of Dunne's 'Experiment with Time' which she had been reading.

Her letter arrived Monday. As I picked it up, I had a sudden sense of depression. However, when I read it, she said I could have the house and told me where to get the keys.

Instead of being cheerful, I grew still more depressed, so much so I decided there must have been something between the lines which I was getting intuitively. I unfolded the letter and read the first page through and as I turned to the second page, I noticed she had written a postscript on the back of the first sheet. It consisted of an extremely blunt and heavy-handed description of an unlovely trait in my character which I had struggled for years to overcome, and for the past two years I thought I had succeeded.

Yet here it was again, described with clinical exactitude.

I was stunned and desolated. I thought to myself, 'What is this letter trying to tell me? In the first place, she invited me to use her house, as I have been seeing myself in some lovely home during the holidays. In the second place, nothing comes to me except I draw it. And thirdly I have been hearing nothing but good news. So the obvious conclusion is that something in me corresponds to this letter and no matter what it looks like it is good news. I reread the letter and as I did so, I asked, 'What is there here for me to see?'

And then I saw. It started out, 'After our conversation of last week, I feel I can tell you...' and the rest of the page was as studded with 'weres' and 'wases' as currants in a seed cake. A great feeling of elation swept over me.

It was all in the past. The thing I had labored so long to correct was done. I suddenly realized that my friend was a witness to my resurrection. I whirled around the studio, chanting, 'It's all in the past! It is done. Thank you, it is done!'

I gathered all my gratitude up in a big ball of light and shot it straight to you and if you saw a flash of lightning Monday evening shortly after six your time, that was it.

Now, instead of writing a polite letter because it is the correct thing to do, I can write giving sincere thanks for her frankness and thanking her for the loan of her house.

Thank you so much for your teaching, which has made my beloved imagination truly my Saviour."

And now, if any man shall say unto her "Lo, here is Christ, or there" [Matthew 24:23], she will believe it not, for she knows that the Kingdom of God is within her and that she herself must assume full responsibility for the incarnation of her ideal and that nothing but death and resurrection will bring her to it.

She has found her Saviour, her beloved Imagination, forever expanding in the bosom of God.

There is only one reality, and that is Christ – Human Imagination, the inheritance and final achievement of the whole of Humanity.

> *That we... speaking the truth in love, may grow up into Him in all things, which is the head, even Christ.*
> —Ephesians 4:14,15

CHAPTER 7

Creation Is Finished

I am the beginning and the end, there is nothing to come that has not been, and is.
—Ecclesiastes 3:15 ERV

Blake saw all possible human situations as "already-made" states. He saw every aspect, every plot and drama as already worked out as "mere possibilities" as long as we are not in them, but as overpowering realities when we are in them.

He described these states as "Sculptures of Los's Halls".

Distinguish therefore states from Individuals in those States. States change but Individual Identities never change nor cease... The Imagination is not a State.

Said Blake, "It is the Human Existence itself. Affection or Love becomes a State when divided from imagination."

Just how important this is to remember is almost impossible to say, but the moment the individual realizes this for the first time is the most momentous in his life, and to be encouraged to feel this is the highest form of encouragement it is possible to give.

This truth is common to all men, but the consciousness of it – and much more, the self- consciousness of it – is another matter.

The day I realized this great truth – that everything in my world is a manifestation of the mental activity which goes on within me, and that the conditions and circumstances of my life only reflect the state of consciousness with which I am fused – is the most momentous in my life.

But the experience that brought me to this certainty is so remote from ordinary existence, I have long hesitated to tell it, for my reason refused to admit the conclusions to which the experience impelled me. Nevertheless, this experience revealed to me that I am supreme within the circle of my own state of consciousness and that it is the state with which I am identified that determines what I experience.

Therefore it should be shared with all, for to know this is to become free from the world's greatest tyranny, the belief in a second cause.

Blessed are the pure in heart: for they shall see God.
—Matthew 5:8

Blessed are they whose imagination has been so purged of the beliefs in second causes they know that imagination is all, and all is imagination.

One day I quietly slipped from my apartment in New York City into some remote yesteryear's countryside. As I entered the dining room of a large inn, I became fully conscious. I knew that my physical body was immobilized on my bed back in New York.

Yet here I was as awake and as conscious as I have ever been. I intuitively knew that if I could stop the activity of my mind, everything before me would freeze. No sooner was the thought born than the urge to try it possessed me. I felt my head tighten, then thicken to a stillness. My attention concentrated into a crystal-clear focus, and the waitress walking, walked not. And I looked through the window and the leaves falling, fell not. And the family of four eating, ate not. And they lifting the food, lifted it not. Then my attention relaxed, the tightness eased, and of a sudden all moved onward in their course. The leaves fell, the waitress walked and the family ate. Then I understood Blake's vision of the "Sculptures of Los's Halls".

I sent you to reap that whereon ye bestowed no labor.
—John 4:38

Creation is finished.

I am the beginning and the end, there is nothing to come that has not been, and is.
—Ecclesiastes 3:15, ERV

The world of creation is finished and its original is within us.

We saw it before we set forth, and have since been trying to remember it and to activate sections of it. There are infinite views of it. Our task is to get the right view and by determined direction of our attention make it pass in procession before the inner eye. If we assemble the right sequence and experience it in imagination until it has the tone of reality, then we consciously create circumstances.

This inner procession is the activity of imagination that must be consciously directed. We, by a series of mental transformations, become aware of increasing portions of that which already is, and by matching our own mental activity to that portion of creation which we desire to experience, we activate it, resurrect it, and give it life.

This experience of mine not only shows the world as a manifestation of the mental activity of the individual observer, but it also reveals our course of time as jumps of attention between eternal moments. An infinite abyss separates any two moments of ours.

We, by the movements of our attention, give life to the "Sculptures of Los's Halls".

Think of the world as containing an infinite number of states of consciousness from which it could be viewed. Think of these states as rooms or mansions in the House of God [John 14:2], and like the rooms of any house, they are fixed relative to one another.

But think of yourself, the Real Self, the Imaginative You, as the living, moving occupant of God's House.

Each room contains some of Los's Sculptures, with infinite plots and dramas and situations already worked out but not activated.

They are activated as soon as Human Imagination enters and fuses with them. Each represents certain mental and emotional activities. To enter a state, man must consent to the ideas and feelings which it represents.

These states represent an infinite number of possible mental transformations which man can experience. To move into another state or mansion necessitates a change of beliefs.

All that you could ever desire is already present and only waits to be matched by your beliefs.

But it must be matched, for that is the necessary condition by which alone it can be activated and objectified.

Matching the beliefs of a state is the seeking that finds, the knocking to which it is opened, the asking that receives [Matthew 7:8; Luke 11:10]. "Go in and possess the land" [Exodus 6:4;8].

The moment man matches the beliefs of any state, he fuses with it, and this union results in the activation and projection of its plots, plans, dramas, and situations.

It becomes the individual's home from which he views the world. It is his workshop, and, if he is observant, he will see outer reality shaping itself upon the model of his... Imagination.

It is for this purpose of training us in image-making that we were made subject to the limitations of the senses and clothed in bodies of flesh.

It is the awakening of the imagination, the returning of His Son, that our Father waits for.

> *The creature was made subject to vanity not willingly, but by reason of him who subjected it.*
> —Romans 8:20

But the victory of the Son, the return of the prodigal, assures us that: "the creature shall be delivered from the bondage of corruption into the glorious liberty of the Sons [children] of God." [Romans 8:21]

We were subjected to this biological experience because no one can know of imagination who has not been subjected to the vanities and limitations of the flesh, who has not taken his share of Sonship and gone prodigal, who has not experimented and tasted this cup of experience; and confusion will continue until man awakes and a fundamentally imaginative view of life has been reestablished and acknowledged as basic.

> *I should preach... the unsearchable riches of Christ and make all men see what is the fellowship of the mystery, which from the beginning of the world has been hid in God, Who created all things by Jesus Christ.*
> —Ephesians 3:8,9

Bear in mind that Christ in you is your imagination.

As the appearance of our world is determined by the particular state with which we are fused, so may we determine our fate as individuals by fusing our imaginations with ideals we seek to realize. On the distinction between our states of consciousness depends the distinction between the circumstances and conditions of our lives.

Man, who is free in his choice of state, often cries out to be saved from the state of his choice.

> *And ye shall cry out in that day, because of your king which ye shall have chosen you; and the Lord will not hear you in that day. Nevertheless, the people refused to obey the voice of Samuel; and they said, Nay; but we will have a king over us.*
> —1 Samuel 8:18,19

Choose wisely the state that you will serve. All states are lifeless until imagination fuses with them.

> *All things when they are admitted are made manifest by the light: for everything that is made manifest is light,*
> —Ephesians 5:13

and

Ye are the light of the world

—Matthew 5:14

by which those ideas to which you have consented are made manifest.

Hold fast to your ideal. Nothing can take it from you but your imagination.

Don't think of your ideal, think from it. It is only the ideals from which you think that are ever realized."

"Man lives not by bread alone, but by every word that proceeds out of the mouth of God.

—Matthew 4:4

and "the mouth of God" is the mind of man.

Become a drinker and an eater of the ideals you wish to realize. Have a set, definite aim or your mind will wander, and wandering it eats every negative suggestion.

If you live right mentally, everything else will be right.

By a change of mental diet, you can alter the course of observed events.

But unless there is a change of mental diet, your personal history remains the same. You illuminate or darken your life by the ideas to which you consent.

Nothing is more important to you than the ideas on which you feed. And you feed on the ideas from which you think. If you find the world unchanged, it is a sure sign that you are wanting in fidelity to the new mental diet, which you neglect in order to condemn your environment. You are in need of a new and sustained attitude.

You can be anything you please if you will make the conception habitual, for any idea which excludes all others from the field of attention discharges in action.

The ideas and moods to which you constantly return define the state with which you are fused.

Therefore train yourself to occupy more frequently the feeling of your wish fulfilled.

This is creative magic. It is the way to work toward fusion with the desired state.

If you would assume the feeling of your wish fulfilled more frequently, you would be master of your fate, but unfortunately you shut out your assumption for all but the occasional hour. Practice making real to yourself the feeling of the wish fulfilled.

After you have assumed the feeling of the wish fulfilled, do not close the experience as you would a book, but carry it around like a fragrant odor.

Instead of being completely forgotten, let it remain in the atmosphere communicating its influence automatically to your actions and reactions. A mood, often repeated, gains a momentum that is hard to break or check. So be careful of the feelings you entertain. Habitual moods reveal the state with which you are fused.

It is always possible to pass from thinking of the end you desire to realize, to thinking from the end.

But the crucial matter is thinking from the end, for thinking from means unification or fusion with the idea: whereas in thinking of the end, there is always subject and object – the thinking individual and the thing thought. You must imagine yourself into the state of your wish fulfilled, in your love for that state, and in so doing, live and think from it and no more of it. You pass from thinking of to thinking from by centering your imagination in the feeling of the wish fulfilled.

CHAPTER 8

The Apple of God's Eye

What think ye of the Christ? Whose Son is He?
—Matthew 22:42

When this question is asked of you, let your answer be, "Christ is my imagination", and, though I "See not yet all things put under him" [Hebrews 2:8], yet I know that I am Mary from whom sooner or later He shall be born, and eventually "Do all things through Christ" [Philippians 4:13].

The birth of Christ is the awakening of the inner or Second man. It is becoming conscious of the mental activity within oneself, which activity continues whether we are conscious of it or not.

The birth of Christ does not bring any person from a distance, or make anything to be that was not there before. It is the unveiling of the Son of God in man. The Lord "cometh in clouds" [Mark 13:26, Luke 21:27] is the prophet's description of the pulsating rings of golden liquid light on the head of him in whom He awakes. The coming is from within and not from without, as Christ is in us [Romans 8:10; 2 Corinthians 13:3; Galatians 2:20; Galatians 4:19; Colossians 1:27].

This great mystery, "God was manifest in the flesh" [1 Timothy 3:16] begins with Advent, and it is appropriate that the cleansing of the Temple

Which temple ye are...
—1 Corinthians 3:17

stands in the forefront of the Christian mysteries:

The Kingdom of Heaven is within you.
—Luke 17:21

Advent is unveiling the mystery of your being. If you will practice the art of revision by a life lived according to the wise, imaginative use of your inner speech and inner actions, in confidence that by the conscious use of "the power that worketh in us" [Ephesians 3:20], Christ will awake in you; if you believe it, trust it, act upon it; Christ will awake in you. This is Advent.

Great is the mystery, God was manifest in the flesh.
—1 Timothy 3:16

From Advent on, He that toucheth you toucheth the apple of God's eye.
—Zechariah 2:8

FREEDOM FOR ALL

FOREWORD

Public opinion will not long endure a theory which does not work in practice. Today, probably more than ever before, man demands proof of the truth of even his highest ideal. For ultimate satisfaction man must find a principle which is for him a way of life, a principle which he can experience as true.

I believe I have discovered just such a principle in the greatest of all sacred writings, the Bible. Drawn from my own mystical illumination, this book reveals the truth buried within the stories of the old and new testaments alike.

Briefly, the book states that consciousness is the one and only reality, that consciousness is the cause and manifestation is the effect. It draws the reader's attention to this fact constantly, that the reader may always keep first things first.

Having laid the foundation that a change of consciousness is essential to bring about any change of expression, this book explains to the reader a dozen different ways to bring about such a change of consciousness.

This is a realistic and constructive principle that works. The revelation it contains, if applied, will set you free.

CHAPTER 1

The Oneness of God

HEAR, O Israel: the Lord our God is one Lord

Hear, O Israel:
Hear, O man made of the very substance of God:
You and God are one and undivided!

Man, the world, and all within it are conditioned states of the unconditioned one, God. You are this one; you are God conditioned as man. All that you believe God to be, you are; but you will never know this to be true until you stop claiming it of another, and recognize this seeming other to be yourself.

God and man,
spirit and matter,
the formless and the formed,
the creator and the creation,
the cause and the effect —
your Father and you are one.

This one, in whom all conditioned states live and move and have their being, is your I AM — your unconditioned consciousness.

Unconditioned consciousness is God, the one and only reality. By unconditioned consciousness is meant a sense of awareness; a sense of knowing *that* I AM apart from knowing *who* I AM; the consciousness of being, divorced from that which I am conscious of being.

I AM aware of being man, but I need not be man to be aware of being. Before I became aware of being someone, I, unconditioned awareness, was aware of being; and this awareness does not depend upon being someone. I AM self-existent, unconditioned consciousness. I became aware of being someone, and I shall become aware of being someone other than this that I am now aware of being. But I AM eternally aware of being, whether I am unconditioned formlessness or I am conditioned form.

As the conditioned state, I (man), might forget who I am, or where I am, but I cannot forget that I AM.

This knowing that I AM, this awareness of being, is the only reality.

This unconditioned consciousness, the I AM, is that knowing reality in whom all conditioned states – conceptions of myself – begin and end, but which ever remains the unknown knowing being when all the known ceases to be.

All that I have ever believed myself to be, all that I now believe myself to be, and all that I shall ever believe myself to be, are but attempts to know myself – the unknown, undefined reality.

This unknown knowing one, or unconditioned consciousness, is my true being, the one and only reality. I AM the unconditioned reality conditioned as that which I believe myself to be. I AM the believer limited by my beliefs, the knower defined by the known.

The world is my conditioned consciousness objectified. That which I feel and believe to be true of myself is now projected in space as my world. The world – my mirrored self – ever bears witness of the state of consciousness in which I live.

There is no chance or accident responsible for the things that happen to me or the environment in which I find myself. Nor is predestined fate the author of my fortunes or misfortunes. Innocence and guilt are mere words with no meaning to the law of consciousness, except as they reflect the state of consciousness itself.

The consciousness of guilt calls forth condemnation. The consciousness of lack produces poverty.

Man everlastingly objectifies the state of consciousness in which he abides, but he has somehow or other become confused in the interpretation of the law of cause and effect.

He has forgotten that it is the inner state which is the cause of the outer manifestation.

As within, so without.
—"Correspondence", the second of
The Seven Principles of Hermes Trismegistus

And in his forgetfulness, he believes that an outside God has his own peculiar reason for doing things, such reasons being beyond the comprehension of mere man. Or he believes that people are suffering because of past mistakes which have been forgotten by the conscious mind. Or again, that blind chance alone plays the part of God.

One day man will realize that his own I AM-ness is the God he has been seeking throughout the ages, and that his own sense of awareness – his consciousness of being – is the one and only reality.

The most difficult thing for man to really grasp is this: That the "I AM-ness" in himself is God. It is his true being or Father state, the only state he can be sure of. The Son, his conception of himself, is an illusion. He always knows that he IS, but that which he is, is an illusion created by himself (the Father) in an attempt at self-definition.

This discovery reveals that all that I have believed God to be I AM.

I AM the resurrection and the life"
—John 11:25

...is a statement of fact concerning my consciousness, for my consciousness resurrects or makes visibly alive that which I am conscious of being

I AM the door.

—John 10:2, 10:7, 10:9

"All that ever came before me are thieves and robbers.

—John 10:8

...shows me that my consciousness is the one and only entrance into the world of expression; that by assuming the consciousness of being or possessing the thing which I desire to be or possess is the only way by which I can become it or possess it; that any attempt to express this desirable state in ways other than by assuming the consciousness of being or possessing it, is to be robbed of the joy of expression and possession.

I AM the beginning and the end.

—Revelation 1:8, 22:13

...reveals my consciousness as the cause of the birth and death of all expression.

I AM hath sent me.

—Exodus 3:14

...reveals my consciousness to be the Lord which sends me into the world in the image and likeness of that which I am conscious of being to live in a world composed of all that I am conscious of.

I AM the Lord, and there is no God beside Me.

—Isaiah 45:5

...declares my consciousness to be the one and only Lord and beside my consciousness there is no God.

BE still and know that I AM God.

—Psalm 46:1

...means that I should still the mind and know that consciousness is God.

> *Thou shalt not take the Name of the Lord thy God in vain.*
> —Exodus 20:7

> "*I AM the Lord: that is My Name.*
> —Isaiah 42:8

Now that you have discovered your I AM, your consciousness to be God, do not claim anything to be true of yourself that you would not claim to be true of God, for in defining yourself, you are defining God.

That which you are conscious of being is that which you have named God. God and man are one. You and your Father are one [John 10:30].

Your unconditioned consciousness, or I AM, and that which you are conscious of being, are one.

The conceiver and the conception are one. If your conception of yourself is less than that which you claim as true of God, you have robbed God [see Philippians 2:6], the Father, because you (the Son or conception) bear witness of the Father or conceiver. Do not take the magical name of God, I AM, in vain for you will not be held guiltless; you must express all that you claim yourself to be.

Name God by consciously defining yourself as your highest ideal.

CHAPTER 2

The Name of God

It cannot be stated too often that consciousness is the one and only reality, for this is the truth that sets man free.

This is the foundation upon which the whole structure of biblical literature rests. The stories of the Bible are all mystical revelations written in an Eastern symbolism which reveals to the intuitive the secret of creation and the formula of escape. The Bible is man's attempt to express in words the cause and manner of creation. Man discovered that his consciousness was the cause or creator of his world, so he proceeded to tell the story of creation in a series of symbolical stories known to us today as the Bible.

To understand this greatest of books, you need a little intelligence and much intuition – intelligence enough to enable you to read the book, and intuition enough to interpret and understand what you read.

You may ask why was the Bible written symbolically. Why was it not written in a clear, simple style so that all who read it might understand it? To these questions I reply that all men speak symbolically to that part of the world which differs from their own.

The language of the West is clear to us of the West, but it is symbolic to the East; and vice versa. An example of this can be found in the Easterner's instruction:

If thine hand offend thee, cut it off.

—Mark 9:43

He speaks of the hand, not as the hand of the body, but as any form of expression; and thereby he warns you to turn from that expression in your world which is offensive to you.

At the same time, the man of the West would unintentionally mislead the man of the East by saying: "This bank is on the rocks." For the expression "on the rocks" to the Westerner is equivalent to bankruptcy, while a rock to an Easterner is a symbol of faith and security.

> *I will like him unto a wise man which built his house upon a rock; and the rain descended, and the floods came, and the winds blew and beat upon that house; and it fell not; for it was founded upon a rock.*
> —Matthew 7:24,25

To really understand the message of the Bible you must bear in mind that it was written by the Eastern mind and therefore cannot be taken literally by those of the West. Biologically, there is no difference between the East and the West. Love and hate are the same; hunger and thirst are the same; ambition and desire are the same; but the technique of expression is vastly different.

The first thing you must discover if you would unlock the secret of the Bible, is the meaning of the symbolic name of the creator which is known to all as Jehovah. This word "Jehovah" is composed of the four Hebrew letters – JOD HE VAU HE. The whole secret of creation is concealed within this name.

The first letter, JOD, represents the absolute state or consciousness unconditioned; the sense of undefined awareness; that all inclusiveness out of which all creation or conditioned states of consciousness come.

In the terminology of today JOD is I AM, or unconditioned consciousness.

The second letter, HE, represents the only begotten Son, a desire, an imaginary state. It symbolizes an idea; a defined subjective state or clarified mental picture.

The third letter, VAU, symbolizes the act of unifying or joining the conceiver (JOD), the consciousness desiring to the conception (HE), the state desired, so that the conceiver and the conception become one.

Fixing a mental state, consciously defining yourself as the state desired, impressing upon yourself the fact that you are now that which you imagined or conceived as your objective, is the function of VAU. It nails or joins the consciousness desiring to the thing desired. The cementing or joining process is accomplished subjectively by feeling the reality of that which is not yet objectified.

The fourth letter, HE, represents the objectifying of this subjective agreement. The JOD HE VAU makes man or the manifested world (HE), in the image and likeness of itself, the subjective conscious state. So the function of the final HE is to objectively bear witness to the subjective state JOD HE VAU.

Conditioned consciousness continually objectifies itself on the screen of space.

The world is the image and likeness of the subjective conscious state which created it.

The visible world of itself can do nothing; it only bears record of is creator, the subjective state. It is the visible Son (HE) bearing witness of the invisible Father, Son and Mother – JOD HE VAU – a Holy Trinity which can only be seen when made visible as man or manifestation.

Your unconditioned consciousness (JOD) is your I AM which visualizes or imagines a desirable state (HE), and then becomes conscious of being that state imagined by feeling and believing itself to be the imagined state. The conscious union between you who desire and that which you desire to be, is made possible through the VAU, or your capacity to feel and believe.

Believing is simply living in the feeling of actually being the state imagined – by assuming the consciousness of being the state desired. The subjective state symbolized as JOD HE VAU then objectifies itself as HE, thereby completing the mystery of the creator's name and nature, JOD HE VAU HE (Jehovah).

JOD is to be aware; HE is to be aware of something; VAU is to be aware as, or to be aware of being that which you were only aware of. The second HE is your visible objectified world which is made in the image and likeness of the JOD HE VAU, or that which you are aware of being.

And God said, Let Us make man in Our image, after Our likeness.
—Genesis 1:26

Let us, JOD HE VAU make the objective manifestation (HE) in our image, the image of the subjective state.

The world is the objectified likeness of the subjective conscious state in which consciousness abides.

This understanding that consciousness is the one and only reality is the foundation of the Bible.

The stories of the Bible are attempts to reveal in symbolic language the secret of creation as well as to show man the one formula to escape from all of his own creations.

This is the true meaning of the name of Jehovah, the name by which all things are made and without which there is nothing made that is made [John 1:3].

First, you are aware; then you become aware of something; then you become aware as that which you were aware of; then you behold objectively that which you are aware of being.

CHAPTER 3

The Law of Creation

Let us take one of the stories of the Bible and see how the prophets and writers of old revealed the story of creation by this strange Eastern symbolism.

We all know the story of Noah and the Ark; that Noah was chosen to create a new world after the world was destroyed by the flood.

The Bible tells us that Noah had three sons, Shem, Ham and Japheth [Genesis 6:10].

The first son is called Shem, which means name. Ham, the second son, means warm, alive. The third son is called Japheth, which means extension. You will observe that Noah and his three sons Shem, Ham and Japheth contain the same formula of creation as does the divine name of JOD HE VAU HE.

Noah, the Father, the conceiver, the builder of a new world is equivalent to the JOD, or unconditioned consciousness, I AM. Shem is your desire; that which you are conscious of; that which you name and define as your objective, and is equivalent to the second letter in the divine name (HE). Ham is the warm, live state of feeling, which joins or binds together consciousness desiring and the thing desired, and is therefore equivalent to the third letter in the divine name, the VAU. The last son, Japheth, means extension, and is the extended or objectified state bearing witness of the subjective state and is equivalent to the last letter in the divine name, HE.

You are Noah, the knower, the creator.

The first thing you beget is an idea, an urge, a desire, the word, or your first son Shem (name).

Your second son Ham (warm, alive) is the secret of FEELING by which you are joined to your desire subjectively so that you, the consciousness desiring, become conscious of being or possessing the thing desired.

Your third son, Japheth, is the confirmation, the visible proof that you know the secret of creation.

He is the extended or objectified state bearing witness of the invisible or subjective state in which you abide.

In the story of Noah it is recorded that Ham saw the secrets of his Father [Genesis 9:22], and, because of his discovery, he was made to serve his brothers, Shem and Japheth [9:25]. Ham, or feeling, is the secret of the Father, your I AM, for it is through feeling that the consciousness desiring is joined to the thing desired.

The conscious union or mystical marriage is made possible only through feeling.

It is feeling which performs this heavenly union of Father and Son, Noah and Shem, unconditioned consciousness and conditioned consciousness.

By performing this service, feeling automatically serves Japheth, the extended or expressed state, for there can be no objectified expression unless there is first a subjective impression.

To feel the presence of the thing desired, to subjectively actualize a state by impressing upon yourself, through feeling, a definite conscious state is the secret of creation.

Your present objectified world is Japheth which was made visible by Ham. Therefore Ham serves his brothers Shem and Japheth, for without feeling which is symbolized as Ham, the idea or thing desired (Shem) could not be made visible as Japheth.

The ability to feel the unseen, the ability to actualize and make real a definite subjective state through the sense of feeling is the secret of creation, the secret by which the word or unseen desire is made visible – is made flesh [John 1:14]. "And God calleth things that be not as though they were" [Romans 4:17].

Consciousness calls things that are not seen as though they were, and it does this by first defining itself as that which it desires to express, and second by remaining within the defined state until the invisible becomes visible.

Here is the perfect working of the law according to the story of Noah. This very moment you are aware of being. This awareness of being, this knowing that you are, is Noah, the creator.

Now with Noah's identity established as your own consciousness of being, name something that you would like to possess or express; define some objective (Shem), and with your desire clearly defined, close your eyes and feel that you have it or are expressing it.

Don't question how it can be done; simply feel that you have it. Assume the attitude of mind that would be yours if you were already in possession of it so that you feel that it is done.

Feeling is the secret of creation.

Be as wise as Ham and make this discovery that you too may have the joy of serving your brothers Shem and Japheth; the joy of making the word or name flesh.

CHAPTER 4

The Secret of Feeling

The secret of feeling or the calling of the invisible into visible states is beautifully told in the story of Isaac blessing his second son Jacob by the belief, based solely upon feeling, that he was blessing his first son Esau.

—Genesis 27:1-35

It is recorded that Isaac, who was old and blind, felt that he was about to leave this world and wishing to bless his first son Esau before he died, sent Esau hunting for savory venison with the promise that upon his return from the hunt he would receive his father's blessing.

Now Jacob, who desired the birthright or right to be born through the blessing of his father, overheard his blind father's request for venison and his promise to Esau. So, as Esau went hunting for the venison, Jacob killed and dressed a kid of his father's flock.

Placing the skins upon his smooth body to give him the feel of his hairy and rough brother Esau, he brought the tastily prepared kid to his blind father Isaac. And Isaac who depended solely upon his sense of feel mistook his second son Jacob for his first son Esau, and pronounced his blessing on Jacob. Esau on his return from the hunt learned that his smooth-skinned brother Jacob had supplanted him so he appealed to his father for justice; but Isaac answered and said:

Thy brother came with subtlety and hath taken away thy blessing.
—Isaiah 27:35

"*I have made him thy Lord, and all his brethren have I given to him for servants.*
—Isaiah 27:37

Simple human decency should tell man that this story cannot be taken literally. There must be a message for man hidden somewhere in this treacherous and despicable act of Jacob! The hidden message, the formula of success buried in this story was intuitively revealed to the writer in this manner. Isaac, the blind father, is your consciousness; your awareness of being.

Esau, the hairy son, is your present objectified world – the rough or sensibly felt; the present moment; the present environment; your present conception of yourself; in short, the world you know by reason of your objective senses. Jacob, the smooth-skinned lad, the second son, is your desire or subjective state, an idea not yet embodied, a subjective state which is perceived and sensed but not objectively known or seen; a point in time and space removed from the present. In short, Jacob is your defined objective. The smooth-skinned Jacob — or subjective state seeking embodiment or the right of birth — when properly felt or blessed by his father (when consciously felt and fixed as real) becomes objectified; and in so doing he supplants the rough, hairy Esau — or the former objectified state. Two things cannot occupy a given place at one and the same time, and so as the invisible is made visible, the former visible state vanishes.

Your consciousness is the cause of your world. The conscious state in which you abide determines the kind of world in which you live. Your present concept of yourself is now objectified as your environment, and this state is symbolized as Esau, the hairy, of sensibly felt; the first son. That which you would like to be or possess is symbolized as your second son, Jacob, the smooth-skinned lad who is not yet seen but is subjectively senses and felt, and will, if properly touched, supplant his brother Esau, or your present world.

Always bear in mind the fact that Isaac, the father of these two sons, or states, is blind. He does not see his smooth-skinned son Jacob; he only feels him.

And through the sense of feeling he actually believes Jacob, the subjective, to be Esau, the real, the objectified.

You do not see your desire objectively; you simply sense it (feel it) subjectively.

You do not grope in space after a desirable state. Like Isaac, you sit still and send your first son hunting by removing your attention from your objective world.

Then in the absence of your first son, Esau, you invite the desirable state, your second son, Jacob, to come close so that you may feel it. "Come close, my son, that I may feel you" [27:21]. First, you are aware of it in your immediate environment; then you draw it closer and closer and closer until you sense it and feel it in your immediate presence so that it is real and natural to you.

> *If two of you shall agree on earth as touching on any point that they shall ask, it shall be done for them of My Father, Which is in heaven.*
>
> —Matthew 18:19

The two agree through the sense of feel; and the agreement is established on earth — is objectified, is made real.

The two agreeing are Isaac and Jacob — you and that which you desire. And the agreement is made solely on the sense of feeling.

Esau symbolizes your present objectified world whether it be pleasant or otherwise.

Jacob symbolizes any and every desire of your heart.

Isaac symbolizes your true self – with your eyes closed to the present world – in the act of sensing and feeling yourself to be or to possess that which you desire to be or to possess.

The secret of Isaac – the sensing, feeling state – is simply the act of mentally separating the sensibly felt (your present physical state) from the insensibly felt (that which you would like to be).

With the objective senses tightly shut Isaac made, and you can make the insensibly felt (the subjective state) seem real or sensibly known, for faith is knowledge.

Knowing the law of self-expression, the law by which the invisible is made visible, is not enough.

It must be applied; and this is the method of application.

First: Send your first son Esau – your present objectified world or problem – hunting. This is accomplished simply by closing your eyes and taking your attention away from the objectified limitations. As your senses are removed from your objective world, it vanishes from your consciousness or goes hunting.

Second: With your eyes still closed and your attention removed from the world round about you, consciously fix the natural time and place for the realization of your desire.

With your objective senses closed to your present environment you can sense and feel the reality of any point in time or space, for both are psychological and can be created at will.

It is vitally important that the natural time-space condition of Jacob, that is, the natural time and place for the realization of your desire be first fixed in your consciousness.

If Sunday is the day on which the thing desired is to be realized, then Sunday must be fixed in consciousness now.

Simply begin to feel that it is Sunday until the quietness and naturalness of Sunday is consciously established.

You have definite associations with the days, weeks, months and seasons of the year. You have said time and again, "Today feels like Sunday, or Monday, or Saturday" or "This feels like Spring, or summer, or Fall, or Winter." This should convince you that you have definite, conscious impressions that you associate with the days, weeks, and seasons of the year.

Then because of these associations you can select any desirable time, and by recalling the conscious impression associated with such time, you can make a subjective reality of that time now.

Do the same with space. If the room in which you are seated is not the room in which the thing desired would be naturally placed or realized, feel yourself seated in the room or place where it would be natural. Consciously fix this time space impression before you start the act of sensing and feeling the nearness, the reality, and the possession of the thing desired. It matters not whether the place desired be ten thousand miles away or only next door, you must fix in consciousness the fact that right where you are seated is the desired place.

You do not make a mental journey; you collapse space. Sit quietly where you are and make "there-ness" "here-ness." Close your eyes and feel that the very place where you are is the place desired. Feel and sense the reality of it until you are consciously impressed with this fact, for your knowledge of this fact is based solely on your subjective sensing.

Third: In the absence of Esau (the problem) and with the natural time-space established, you invite Jacob (the solution) to come and fill this space – to come and supplant his brother.

In your imagination see the thing desired. If you cannot visualize it, sense the general outline of it; contemplate it. Then mentally draw it close to you. "Come close, my son, that I may feel you."

Feel the nearness of it. Feel it to be in your immediate presence. Feel the reality and solidity of it. Feel it and see it naturally placed in the room in which you are seated. Feel the thrill of actual accomplishment and the joy of possession.

Now open your eyes. This brings you back to the objective world – the rough or sensibly felt world. Your hairy son Esau has returned from the hunt and by his very presence tells you that you have been betrayed by your smooth-skinned son Jacob – the subjective, psychologically felt.

But like Isaac, whose confidence was based upon the knowledge of this changeless law, you too will say, "I have made him thy Lord and all his brethren have I given to him for servants".

That is, even though your problems appears fixed and real, you have felt the subjective, psychological state to be real to the point of receiving the thrill of that reality. You have experienced the secret of creation for you have felt the reality of the subjective.

You have fixed a definite psychological state which in spite of all opposition or precedent will objectify itself, thereby fulfilling the name of Jacob – the supplanter.

Here are a few practical examples of this drama.

First: The blessing or making a thing real.

Sit in your living room and name a piece of furniture, rug or lamp that you would like to have in this particular room. Look at that area of the room where you would place it if you had it. Close your eyes and let all that now occupies that area of the room vanish. In your imagination see this area as empty space – there is absolutely nothing there. Now begin to fill this space with the desired piece of furniture. Sense and feel that you have it in this very area. Imagine you are seeing that which you desired to see. Continue in this consciousness until you feel the thrill of possession.

Second: The blessing or the making of a place real.

You are now seated in your apartment in New York City, contemplating the joy that would be yours if you were on an ocean liner sailing across the great Atlantic.

> *I go to prepare a place for you. And if I go and prepare a place for you, I will come again, and receive you unto myself; that where I am there ye may be also.*
>
> —John 14:2-3

Your eyes are closed; you have consciously released the New York apartment and in its place you sense and feel that you are on an ocean liner. You are seated in a deck chair; there is nothing round you but the vast Atlantic. Fix the reality of this ship and ocean so that in this state you can mentally recall the day when you were seated in your New York apartment dreaming of this day at sea. Recall the mental picture of yourself seated there in New York dreaming of this day. In your imagination see the memory picture of yourself back there in your New York apartment. If you succeed in looking back on your New York apartment without consciously returning there, then you have successfully prepared the reality of this voyage.

Remain in this conscious state feeling the reality of the ship and the ocean; feel the joy of this accomplishment – then open your eyes.

You have gone and prepared the place; you have fixed a definite psychological state and where you are in consciousness there you shall be in body also.

Third: The blessing or making real of a point in time.

You consciously let go of this day, month or year, as the case may be, and you imagine that it is now that day, month or year which you desire to experience. You sense and feel the reality of the desired time by impressing upon yourself the fact that it is now accomplished. As you sense the naturalness of this time, you begin to feel the thrill of having fully realized that which before you started this psychological journey in time you desired to experience at this time.

With the knowledge of your power to bless you can open the doors of any prison – the prison of illness or poverty or of a humdrum existence.

> *The Spirit of the Lord God is upon me; because the Lord hath anointed me to preach good tidings unto the meek; he hath sent me to bind up the broken hearted, to proclaim liberty to the captives, and the opening of the prison to them that are bound.*
>
> —Isaiah 61:1, Luke 4:18

CHAPTER 5

The Sabbath

Six days shall work be done, but on the seventh day their shall be to you an holy day, a Sabbath of rest to the Lord.
—Exodus 31:15, Leviticus 23:3

These six days are not twenty-four hour periods of time. They symbolize the psychological moment a definite subjective state is fixed.

These six days of work are subjective experiences, and consequently cannot be measured by sidereal time, for the real work of fixing a definite psychological state is done in consciousness.

The time spent in consciously defining yourself as that which you desire to be is the measure of these six days.

A change of consciousness is the work done in these six creative days; a psychological adjustment, which is measured not by sidereal time but by actual (subjective) accomplishment. Just as a life in retrospect is measured not by years but by the content of those years, so too is this psychological interval measured, not by the time spent in making the adjustment, but by the accomplishment of that interval.

The true meaning of six days of work (creation) is revealed in the mystery of the VAU, which is the sixth letter in the Hebrew alphabet, and the third letter in the divine name: JOD HE VAU HE.

As previously explained in the mystery of the name of Jehovah, VAU means to nail or join.

The creator is joined to his creation through feeling; and the time that it takes you to fix a definite feeling is the true measure of these six days of creation.

Mentally separating yourself from the objective world and attaching yourself through the secret of feeling to the subjective state is the function of the sixth letter of the Hebrew alphabet, VAU, or the six days of work.

There is always an interval between the fixed impression, or subjective state, and the outward expression of that state.

The interval is called the Sabbath.

The Sabbath is the mental rest which follows the fixed psychological state. It is the result of your six days of work.

The Sabbath was made for man.
—Mark 2:27

This mental rest which follows a successful conscious impregnation is the period of mental pregnancy, a period which is made for the purpose of incubating the manifestation.

It was made for the manifestation; the manifestation was not made for it.

Automatically you keep the Sabbath a day of rest — a period of mental rest — if you succeed in accomplishing your six days of work.

There can be no Sabbath, no seventh day, no period of mental rest, until the six days are over — until the psychological adjustment is accomplished and the mental impression is fully made.

Man is warned that if he fails to keep the Sabbath, if he fails to enter into the rest of God, he will also fail to receive the promise; he will fail to realize his desires.

The reason for this is simple and obvious. There can be no mental rest until a conscious impression is made.

If a man fails to fully impress upon himself the fact that he now has that which heretofore he desired to possess, he will continue to desire it, and therefore he will not be mentally at rest or satisfied.

If, on the other hand, he succeeds in making this conscious adjustment so that upon emerging from the period of silence or his subjective six days of work, he knows by his feeling that he has the thing desired, then he automatically enters the Sabbath or the period of mental rest.

Pregnancy follows impregnation. Man does not continue desiring that which he has already acquired. The Sabbath can be kept as a day of rest only after man succeeds in becoming conscious of being that which before entering the silence he desired to be.

The Sabbath is the result of the six days of work.

The man who knows the true meaning of these six work days realizes that the observance of one day of the week as a day of physical quietness is not keeping the Sabbath.

The peace and the quiet of the Sabbath can be experienced only when man has succeeded in becoming conscious of being that which he desires to be. If he fails to make this conscious impression he has missed the mark. He has sinned, for to sin is to miss the mark, to fail to achieve one's objective; a state in which there is no peace of mind.

If I had not come and spoken unto them, they had not had sin.

—John 15:22

If man had not been presented with an ideal state toward which to aim, a state to be desired and acquired, he would have been satisfied with his lot in life and would never have known sin.

Now that man knows that his capacities are infinite, knows that by working six days or by making a psychological adjustment he can realize his desires, he will not be satisfied until he achieves his every objective.

He will, with the true knowledge of these six work days, define his objective and set about becoming conscious of being it.

When this conscious impression is made it is automatically followed by a period of mental rest, a period the mystic calls the

Sabbath, an interval in which the conscious impression will be gestated and physically expressed.

The word will be made flesh. But that is not the end!

The Sabbath, or rest which will be broken by the embodiment of the idea, will sooner or later give way to another six days of work as man defines another objective and begins anew the act of defining himself as that which he desires to be.

Man has been stirred out of his sleep through the medium of desire, and can find no rest until he realizes his desire.

But before he can enter into the rest of God, or keep the Sabbath, before he can walk unafraid and at peace, he must become a good spiritual marksman and learn the secret of hitting the mark or working six days — the secret by which he lets go the objective state and adjusts himself to the subjective.

This secret was revealed in the divine name Jehovah, and again in the story of Isaac blessing his son Jacob. If man will apply the formula as it is revealed on these Bible dramas he will hit a spiritual bull's eye every time, for he will know that the mental rest or Sabbath is entered only as he succeeds in making a psychological adjustment.

The story of the crucifixion beautifully dramatizes these six days (psychological period) and the seventh day of rest.

It is recorded that it was the custom of the Jews to have someone released from prison at the feast of the Passover, and that they were given the choice of having released unto them either Barabbas the robber, or Jesus the savior. And they cried, "Release Barabbas" [John 18:40]. Whereupon Barabbas was released and Jesus was crucified.

It is further recorded that Jesus the Savior was crucified on the sixth day, entombed or buried on the seventh, and resurrected on the first day.

The savior in your case is that which would save you from that which you are not conscious of being, while Barabbas the thief is your present conception of yourself which robs you of that which you would like to be.

In defining your savior you define that which would save you and not how you would be saved.

Your savior or desire has ways ye know not of; his ways are past finding out [Romans 11:33].

Every problem reveals its own solution. If you were imprisoned you would automatically desire to be free. Freedom, then, is the thing that would save you. It is your savior.

Having discovered your savior the next step in this great drama of the resurrection is to release Barabbas, the robber — your present concept of yourself — and to crucify your savior — or fix the consciousness of being or having that which would save you.

Barabbas represents your present problem. Your savior is that which would free you from this problem. You release Barabbas by taking your attention away from your problem, away from your sense of limitation, for it robs you of the freedom that you seek. And you crucify your savior by fixing a definite psychological state by feeling that you are free from the limitation of the past.

You deny the evidence of the senses and begin to feel subjectively the joy of being free. You feel this state of freedom to be so real that you too cry out, "I am free!" "It is finished." [John 19:30].

The fixing of this subjective state — the crucifixion - takes place on the sixth day. Before the sun sets on this day you must have completed the fixation by feeling, "It is so," "It is finished."

The subjective knowing is followed by the Sabbath or mental rest. You will be as one buried or entombed, for you will know that no matter how mountainous the barriers, how impassable the walls appear to be, your crucified and buried savior (your present subjective fixation) will resurrect himself. By keeping the Sabbath a period of mental rest, by assuming the attitude of mind that would be yours if you were already visibly expressing this freedom, you will receive the promise of the Lord. For the Word will be made flesh — the subjective fixation will embody itself.

And God did rest the seventh day from all His works.
—Hebrews 4:4

Your consciousness is God resting in the knowledge that, "It is well," "It is finished." And your objective senses shall confirm that it is so for the day shall reveal it.

CHAPTER 6

Healing

The formula for the cure of leprosy as revealed in the fourteenth chapter of Leviticus is most illuminating when viewed through the eyes of a mystic. This formula can be prescribed as the positive cure of any disease in man's world, be it physical, mental, financial, social, moral — anything.

It matters not about the nature of the disease or its duration, for the formula can be successfully applied to any and all of them.

Here is the formula as it is recorded in the book of Leviticus:

> *Then shall the priest command to take for him that is to be cleansed two birds alive and clean... and the priest shall command that one of the birds be killed.... As for the living bird, he shall take it and shall dip it in the blood of the bird that was killed; and he shall sprinkle upon him that is to be cleansed from the leprosy seven times and shall pronounce him clean and shall let the living bird loose into the open field.... And he shall be clean.*
>
> —Lev. 14:4-8

A literal application of this story would be stupid and fruitless, while on the other hand, a psychological application of the formula is wise and fruitful.

A bird is a symbol of an idea. Every man who has a problem or who desires to express something other than that which he is now expressing can be said to have two birds.

These two birds or conceptions can be defined as follows:

The first bird is your present, out-pictured conception of yourself; it is the description which you would give if you were asked to define yourself – your physical condition, your income, your obligations, your nationality, family, race, and so on. Your sincere answer to these questions would necessarily be based solely upon the evidence of your senses and not upon any wishful thinking.

This true conception of yourself (based entirely upon the evidences of your senses) defines the first bird.

The second bird is defined by the answer you wish you might give in these questions of self-definition. In short, these two birds can be defined as that which you are conscious of being and that which you desire to be.

Another definition of the two birds would be the first, your present problem regardless of its nature; and the second, the solution to that problem.

For example, if you were sick, good health would be the solution. If you were in debt, freedom from debt would be the solution. If you were hungry, food would be the solution. As you have noticed, the how, the manner of realizing the solution, is not considered. Only the problem and the solution are considered.

Every problem reveals its own solution. For sickness it is health; for poverty it is riches; for weakness it is strength; for confinement it is freedom.

These two states then, your problem and its solution, are the two birds you bring to the priest. You are the priest who now performs the drama of the curing of the man of leprosy — you and your problem. You are the priest; and with the formula for the cure of leprosy you now free yourself from your problem.

First: Take one of the birds (your problem) and kill it by extracting the blood from it. Blood is man's consciousness.

He hath made of one blood all nations of men to dwell on all the face of the earth.

—Acts 17:26

Your consciousness is the one and only reality which animates and makes real that which you are conscious of being. So turning your attention away from the problem is equivalent to extracting the blood from the bird. Your consciousness is the one blood which makes all states living realities. By removing your attention from any given state you have drained the lifeblood from that state. You kill or eliminate the first bird (your problem) by removing your attention from it. Into this blood (your consciousness) you dip the live bird (the solution), or that which heretofore you desired to be or possess. This you do by freeing yourself to be the desirable state now.

The dipping of the live bird into the blood of the bird that was killed is similar to the blessing of Jacob by his blind father Isaac. As you recall, blind Isaac could not see his objective world, his son Esau. You too are blind to your problem, the first bird; for you have removed your attention from it and therefore you do not see it. Your attention (blood) is now placed upon the second bird (subjective state), and you feel and sense the reality of it.

Seven times you are told to sprinkle the one to be cleansed. This means you must dwell within the new conception of yourself until you mentally enter the seventh day (the Sabbath), until the mind is stilled or fixed in the belief that you are actually expressing or possessing that which you desire to be or to possess. At the seventh sprinkle you are instructed to lose the living bird and pronounce the man clean.

As you fully impress upon yourself the fact that you are that which you desire to be, you have symbolically sprinkled yourself seven times; then you are as free as the bird that is loosed. And like the bird in flight which must in a little while return to the earth, so must your subjective impressions or claim in a little while embody itself in your world.

This story and all the other stories of the Bible are psychological plays dramatized within the consciousness of man.

You are the high priest. You are the leper. You are the birds.

Your consciousness or I AM is the high priest. You, the man with the problem, are the leper. The problem, your present concept of yourself, is the bird that is killed. The solution of the problem, what you desire to be, is the living bird that is freed.

You re-enact this great drama within yourself by turning your attention away from your problem and placing it upon that which you desire to express.

You impress upon yourself the fact that you are that which you desire to be until your mind is stilled in the belief that it is so.

Living in this fixed attitude of mind, living in the consciousness that you are now that which you formerly desired to be, is the bird in flight, unfettered by the limitations of the past and moving toward the embodiment of your desire.

CHAPTER 7

Desire, the Word of God

So shall My word be that goeth forth out of My mouth; it shall not return unto Me void, but it shall accomplish that which I please, and it shall prosper in the thing whereunto I sent it.
—Isaiah 55:11

God speaks to you through the medium of your basic desires. Your basic desires are words of promise or prophecies that contain within themselves the plan and power of expression.

By "basic desire" is meant your real objective. Secondary desires deal with the manner of realization. God, your I AM, speaks to you, the conditioned conscious state, through your basic desires. Secondary desires or ways of expression are the secrets of your I AM, the all-wise Father. Your Father, I AM, reveals the first and last: "I am the beginning and the end" [Revelation 1:8, 22:13]; but never does He reveal the middle or secret of His ways. That is, the first is revealed as the word, your basic desire. The last is its fulfillment; the word made flesh. The second or middle (the plan of unfoldment) is never revealed to man, but remains forever the Father's secret.

For I testify unto every man that heareth the words of the prophecy of this book, if any man shall add unto those things, God shall add unto him the plagues that are written in this book; and if any man shall take away from the words of the book of this prophecy, God shall take away his part out of the book of life.

—Rev 22:18-19

The words of prophecy spoken of in the book of Revelation are your basic desires which must not be further conditioned. Man is constantly adding to and taking from these words. Not knowing that the basic desire contains the plan and power of expression, man is always compromising and complicating his desire.

Here is an illustration of what man does to the word of prophecy, his desires.

Man desires freedom from his limitation or problem. The first thing he does after he defines his objective is to condition it upon something else.

He begins to speculate on the manner of acquiring it. Not knowing that the thing desired has a way of expression all of its own he starts planning how he is going to get it, thereby adding to the word of God.

If, on the other hand, he has no plan or conception as to the fulfillment of his desire, then he compromises his desire by modifying it. He feels that if he will be satisfied with less than his basic desire, then he might have a better chance of realizing it. In doing so he takes from the word of God.

Individuals and nations alike are constantly violating this law of their basic desire by plotting and planning the realization of their ambitions; they thereby add to the word of prophecy, or they compromise with their ideals, thus taking from the word of God.

The inevitable result is death and plagues or failure and frustration as promised for such violations.

God speaks to man only through the medium of his basic desires.

Your desires are determined by your conception of yourself. Of themselves, they are neither good or evil.

> *I know and am persuaded by the Lord Christ Jesus that there is nothing unclean of itself but to him that seeth anything to be unclean to him it is unclean.*
> —Romans 14:14

Your desires are the natural and automatic result of your present conception of yourself.

God, your unconditioned consciousness, is impersonal and no respecter of persons [Acts 10:34, Romans 2:11].

Your unconditioned consciousness, God, gives to your conditioned consciousness, man, through the medium of your basic desires that which your conditioned state (your present conception of yourself) believes it needs.

As long as you remain in your present conscious state, so long will you continue desiring that which you now desire.

Change your conception of yourself and you will automatically change the nature of your desires.

Desires are states of consciousness seeking embodiment. They are formed by man's consciousness and can easily be expressed by the man who has conceived them.

Desires are expressed when the man who has conceived them assumes the attitude of mind that would be his if the states desired were already expressed. Now because desires, regardless of their nature, can be so easily expressed by fixed attitudes of mind, a word of warning must be given to those who have not yet realized the oneness of life, and who do not know the fundamental truth that consciousness is God, the one and only reality.

This warning was given to man in the famous Golden Rule:

> *Do unto others that which you would have them do unto you.*
> —Matthew 7:21

You may desire something for yourself or you may desire for another. If your desire concerns another make sure that the thing desired is acceptable to that other. The reason for this warning is that your consciousness is God, the giver of all gifts.

Therefore, that which you feel and believe to be true of another is a gift you have given him. The gift that is not accepted returns to the giver.

Be very sure then that you would love to possess the gift yourself, for if you fix a belief within yourself as true of another and he does not accept this state as true of himself, this unaccepted gift will embody itself within your world.

Always hear and accept as true of others that which you would desire for yourself. In so doing, you are building heaven on earth.

"Do unto others as you would have them do unto you" is based upon this law.

Only accept such states as true of others that you would willingly accept as true of yourself that you may constantly create heaven on earth. Your heaven is defined by the state of consciousness in which you live, which state is made up of all that you accept as true of yourself and true of others.

Your immediate environment is defined by your own conception of yourself plus your convictions regarding others, which have not been accepted by them.

Your conception of another which is not his conception of himself is a gift returned to you.

Suggestions, like propaganda, are boomerangs unless they are accepted by those to whom they are sent.

So your world is a gift you have given to yourself.

The nature of the gift is determined by your conception of yourself plus the unaccepted gifts you offered others.

Make no mistake about this; law is no respecter of persons.

Discover the law of self-expression and live by it; then you will be free. With this understanding of the law, define your desire, know exactly what you want; make certain that it is desirable and acceptable.

The wise and disciplined man sees no barrier to the realization of his desire; he sees nothing to destroy. With a fixed attitude of mind he recognizes that the thing desired is already fully expressed, for he knows that a fixed subjective state has ways and means of expressing itself of which no man knows.

Before they ask I have answered.
—Approx., Isaiah 65:24

"I have ways ye know not of.
—Approx., Isaia 42:16

"My ways are past finding out.
—Romans 11:33

The undisciplined man, on the other hand, constantly sees opposition to the fulfillment of his desire. And because of the frustration, he forms desires of destruction which he firmly believes must be expressed before his basic desire can be realized. When man discovers this law of one consciousness, he will understand the great wisdom of the Golden Rule, and so he will live by it and prove to himself that the kingdom of heaven is on earth.

You will realize why you should "do unto others that which you would have them do unto you." You will know why you should live by this Golden Rule because you will discover that it is just good common sense to do so, since the rule is based upon life's changeless law and is no respecter of persons.

Consciousness is the one and only reality. The world and all within it are states of consciousness objectified.

Your world is defined by your conception of yourself PLUS YOUR CONCEPTIONS OF OTHERS which are not their conceptions of themselves.

The story of the Passover is to help you turn your back on the limitations of the present and pass over into a better and freer state.

The suggestion to "follow the man with the pitcher of water" [Mark 14:13; Luke 22:10] was given to the disciples to guide them to the last supper or the feast of the Passover. The man with the pitcher of water is the eleventh disciple, Simon of Canaan, the disciplined quality of mind which hears only dignified, noble and kindly states.

The mind that is disciplined to hear only the good feasts upon good states and so embodies the good on earth.

If you to would attend the last supper — the great feast of the Passover — then follow this man. Assume this attitude of mind symbolized as the "man with the pitcher of water" and you will live in a world that is really heaven on earth.

The feast of the Passover is the secret of changing your consciousness.

You turn your attention from your present conception of yourself and assume the consciousness of being that which you want to be, thereby passing from one state to another.

This feat is accomplished with the help of the twelve disciples, which are the twelve disciplined qualities of mind [see Your Faith is Your Fortune by the same author, chapter 18].

CHAPTER 8

Faith

And Jesus said unto them, Because of your unbelief; for verily I say unto you, if ye have faith as a grain of mustard seed, ye shall say unto this mountain, remove hence to yonder place; and it shall remove; and nothing shall be impossible unto you.
—Matthew 17:20

This faith of a grain of mustard seed has proved a stumbling block to man [1Corinthians 1:23]. He has been taught to believe that a grain of mustard seed signifies a small degree of faith. So he naturally wonders why he, a mature man, should lack this insignificant measure of faith when so small an amount assures success.

"Faith," he is told, "is the substance of things hoped for, the evidence of things not seen" [Hebrews 11:1]. And again, "Through faith... the worlds were framed by the word of God, so that things which are seen were not made of things which do appear" [Hebrews 11:3].

Invisible things were made visible. The grain of mustard seed is not the measure of a small amount of faith. On the contrary, it is the absolute in faith.

A mustard seed is conscious of being a mustard seed and a mustard seed alone. It is not aware of any other seed in the world. It is sealed in the conviction that it is a mustard seed in the same manner that the spermatozoa sealed in the womb is conscious of being man and only man.

A grain of mustard seed is truly the measure of faith necessary to accomplish your every objective; but like the mustard seed you too must lose yourself in the consciousness of being only the thing desired.

You abide within this sealed state until it bursts itself and reveals your conscious claim.

Faith is feeling or living in the consciousness of being the thing desired. Faith is the secret of creation, the VAU in the divine name JOD HE VAU HE. Faith is the Ham in the family of Noah. Faith is the sense of feeling by which Isaac blessed and made real his son Jacob. By faith, God (your consciousness) calleth things that are not seen as though they were and makes them seen.

It is faith which enables you to become conscious of being the thing desired. Again, it is faith which seals you in this conscious state until your invisible claim ripens to maturity and expresses itself, is made visible.

Faith or feeling is the secret of this appropriation. Through feeling, the consciousness desiring is joined to the thing desired.

How would you feel if you were that which you desire to be?

Wear the mood, this feeling that would be yours if you were already that which you desire to be; and in a little while you will be sealed in the belief that you are. Then without effort this invisible state will objectify itself; the invisible will be made visible.

If you had the faith of a grain of mustard seed you would this day through the magical substance of feeling seal yourself in the consciousness of being that which you desire to be.

In this mental stillness or tomblike state you would remain, confident that you need no one to roll away the stone [Matthew 28:2; Mark 16:3; Luke 24:2; John 20:1]; for all the mountains, stones and inhabitants of earth are nothing in your sight [Isaiah 40:17; Daniel 4:32]. That which you now recognize to be true of yourself (this present conscious state) will do according to its nature among all the inhabitants of earth, and none can stay its hand or say unto it, "What doest Thou?" [Daniel 4:32]. None can stop this conscious state in which you are sealed from embodying itself, nor question its right to be.

This conscious state when properly sealed by faith is a Word of God, I AM, for the man so seated is saying, "I AM so and so," and the Word of God (my fixed conscious state) is spirit and cannot return unto me void but must accomplish whereunto it is sent. God's word (your conscious state) must embody itself that you may know: "I AM the Lord… there is no God beside Me" [Isaiah 45:5]. "The Word was made flesh and dwelt among us" [John 1:14], and "He sent His word and healed him" [Psalm 107:20].

You too can send your word, God's Word, and heal a friend. Is there something that you would like to hear of a friend? Define this something that you know he would love to be or to possess. Now with your desire properly defined you have a Word of God. To send this Word on its way, to speak this Word into being, you simply do this. Sit quietly where you are and assume the mental attitude of listening; recall your friend's voice; with this familiar voice established in your consciousness, imagine that you are actually hearing his voice and that he is telling you that he is or has that which you wanted him to be or to have.

Impress upon your consciousness the fact that you actually heard him and that he told you what you wanted to hear; feel the thrill of having heard. Then drop it completely. This is the mystic's secret of sending words into expression – of making the word flesh. You form within yourself the word, the thing you want to hear; then you listen, and tell it to yourself. "Speak, Lord, for thy servant heareth" [1Samuel 3:9,10].

Your consciousness is the Lord speaking through the familiar voice of a friend and impressing on yourself that which you desire to hear. This self-impregnation, the state impressed upon yourself, the Word, has ways and means of expressing itself of which no man knows. As you succeed in making the impression, you will be unmoved by appearances, for this self-impression is sealed as a grain of mustard seed and will in due season mature to its full expression.

CHAPTER 9

The Annunciator

The use of a friend's voice to impregnate one's self with a desirable state is beautifully told in the story of the Immaculate Conception.

It is recorded that God sent an angel to Mary to announce the birth of his son.

> "And the angel said unto her... thou shalt conceive in thy womb, and bring forth a son... Then said Mary unto the angel, How shall this be, seeing I know not a man? And the angel answered and said unto her, The Holy Ghost shall come upon thee, and the power of the highest shall over-shadow thee; therefore also that holy thing which shall be born of thee shall be called the son of God. For with God nothing shall be impossible.
>
> —Luke 1:30-37

This is the story that has been told for centuries the world over; but man was not told that it was written about himself, so he has failed to receive the benefit it was intended to give him.

The story reveals the method by which the idea or Word was made flesh. God, we are told, germinated or begat an idea, a son, without the aid of another. Then He placed His germinal idea in the womb of Mary with the help of an angel who made the announcement to her and impregnated her with the idea.

No simpler method was ever recorded of consciousness impregnating itself than is found in the story of the Immaculate Conception.

The four characters in this drama of creation are the Father, the Son, Mary, and the Angel.

The Father symbolizes your consciousness. The Son symbolizes your desire. Mary symbolizes your receptive attitude of mind. And the Angel symbolizes the method used to make the impregnation.

The drama unfolds in this manner. The Father begets a Son without the aid of another.

You define your objective; you clarify your desire without the help or suggestion of another.

Then the Father selects that angel who is best qualified to bear this message or germinal possibility to Mary.

You select the person in your world who would be sincerely thrilled in witnessing the fulfillment of your desire.

Then Mary learns through the angel that she has already conceived a Son without the aid of man.

You assume a receptive attitude of mind, a listening attitude, and imagine you are hearing the voice of the one you have chosen to tell you what you desire to know. Imagine that you hear him tell you that you are and have that which you desire to be and to have. You remain in this receptive state until you feel the thrill of having heard the good and wonderful news. Then like Mary of the story, you go about your business in secret, telling no one of this wonderful and immaculate self-impregnation, confident that in due season you will express this impression.

The Father generates the seed or germinal possibility of a Son but in a eugenic impregnation. He does not convey the spermatozoa from Himself to the womb. He has it borne through another medium.

Consciousness desiring is the Father generating the seed or idea. A clarified desire is the perfectly formed seed or the only begotten Son. This seed is then carried from the Father (consciousness desiring) to the Mother (consciousness of being and having the state desired).

This change in consciousness is accomplished by the angel or imaginary voice of a friend telling you that you have already achieved your objective.

The use of an angel or friend's voice to make a conscious impression is the shortest, safest and surest way to be self-impregnated.

With your desire properly defined, you assume an attitude of listening. Imagine you are hearing the voice of a friend; then make him tell you (imagine he is telling you) how lucky and fortunate you are to have fully realized your desire.

In this receptive attitude of mind you are receiving the message of an angel; you are receiving the impression that you are and have that which you desire to be and to have. The emotional thrill of having heard that which you desire to hear is the moment of conception. It is the moment you become self-impregnated, the moment you actually feel you are now that or have that which heretofore you but desired to be or to possess.

As you emerge from this subjective experience, you, like Mary of the story, will know by your changed attitude of mind that you have conceived a Son; that you have fixed a definite subjective state and will in a little while express or objectify this state.

This book has been written to show you how to achieve your objectives. Apply the principle expressed herein and all the inhabitants of earth cannot stop you from realizing your desires.

www.ingramcontent.com/pod-product-compliance
Lightning Source LLC
LaVergne TN
LVHW091539070526
838199LV00002B/125